Spirit Allies & Healing Guides

About the Author

Dawn McLaughlin graduated from Minot State University with a degree in mathematics but has always been fascinated with metaphysical concepts. She is a Reiki healer, tarot reader, astrologer, and hypnotherapist. Dawn lives in Rhode Island with her husband, Kevin, and their lively Italian Greyhound, Dharma. Explore her website at Intuitive-Hearts.com to check out her many offerings.

Spirit Allies & Healing Guides

Create Your
Divine
Support System

Dawn McLaughlin

Llewellyn Publications • Woodbury, Minnesota

First Edition
First Printing, 2024

Cover design by Verlynda Pinckney

Llewellyn Publications is a registered trademark of Llewellyn Worldwide Ltd.

Library of Congress Cataloging-in-Publication Data (Pending)
ISBN: 978-0-7387-7578-4

Llewellyn Worldwide Ltd. does not participate in, endorse, or have any authority or responsibility concerning private business transactions between our authors and the public.

All mail addressed to the author is forwarded but the publisher cannot, unless specifically instructed by the author, give out an address or phone number.

Any internet references contained in this work are current at publication time, but the publisher cannot guarantee that a specific location will continue to be maintained. Please refer to the publisher's website for links to authors' websites and other sources.

Llewellyn Publications
A Division of Llewellyn Worldwide Ltd.
2143 Wooddale Drive
Woodbury, MN 55125-2989
www.llewellyn.com

Printed in the United States of America

Other Books by Dawn McLaughlin

Everyday Reiki (Llewellyn 2023)

Dedication

This book is dedicated to my spirit guides,
who have consistently provided me with sage advice,
encouragement, and limitless inspiration through the years.

Contents

Introduction

There are many facets to who I am and how I define myself. At any given moment, I am a mother, a wife, a mystic, a healer, a writer, a seeker, and a whimsical romantic. As a young child, I was fascinated by occult concepts, ancient civilizations, fantastical creatures, and fairy tales. I spent countless hours playing with my imaginary friends in fantasy lands carefully crafted in my mind's eye.

However, as I transitioned into my teenage years and early adulthood, responsibility took center stage, so I willingly relinquished my relationship with my imagination and the supernatural. Years later, life took its toll: Stress and illness became the hallmarks of my daily life. By my late thirties, I began to search for new answers to the classic questions of life: What is reality? Why am I here? How can I heal?

Determined to find answers and take charge of my life, I began to explore alternative medicine and actively participate in my healing process. I turned to approaches such as reflexology, acupuncture, yoga, meditation, sounding healing, and Reiki. When I began to experience remarkable changes in my life, my curiosity became piqued, so I dove deeper into metaphysical topics. I strove to acquire and integrate this healing knowledge into my daily life.

After my Reiki II training, I had a direct experience with a spirit guide that reminded me of my interactions with my childhood imaginary friends. The encounter was so life-altering that it changed how I view reality and my place in it. I welcomed my newfound spirit team of guides, spirit animal helpers, ancestors, and others with excitement and reverence. I have spent the last ten years cultivating these relationships. I am still in awe of the benefits these allies serve in my personal healing and my ability to assist others with their healing process.

Why I Developed This Book

Modern society routinely dismisses anything that can't be quantified and qualified. Reiki has gained some acceptance as a healing practice in the medical community. Still, the concept of working with spirit allies as part of the healing process may appear too fantastical for some. It can be challenging for most people to determine the difference between an encounter with a spirit guide and a vivid daydream.

I created this comprehensive guide to assist energy workers and those interested in personal healing in learning to access the unseen realms and establish connections with their spirit guides and other high-vibrational beings who can help us achieve our healing goals. Over time, these relationships can blossom into authentic sources of inspiration, knowledge, and healing. This book is suitable for Reiki practitioners of all levels, energy healers, and anyone interested in working with spirit allies for healing on all levels of being—physical, mental, emotional, energetic, and spiritual.

Using This Book

The first part of the book is dedicated to information regarding your spiritual helpers who can assist you on your healing path. You will have the opportunity to reflect on your unique journey and what you hope to accomplish by working with your divine spirit allies. You will be provided with skills and techniques that will assist you with connecting with these spirit beings. The type of spirit allies available to you will be reviewed, along with options for selecting the best members of your Divine Support System to meet your healing goals. Different methods of communication and cultivating relationships will be explored. By the end of chapter 9, you will be empowered to take charge of your healing journey by receiving the assistance of your Divine Support System.

Chapter 10 is an extensive listing of healing deities from across the globe. No single book could chronicle all the healing gods, goddesses, ascended masters, saints, sages, and angels in existence; for one thing, many deities have been lost over the centuries. The selection in this text represents a sampling of the divine beings available to us for inspiration, guidance, and healing. You may feel called to develop relationships with deities associated with your own heritage, the deities of the land where you live, or the gods and goddesses of a different culture entirely. In my experience, deities from other cultures are willing to assist us as long as they are approached with the appropriate reverence and respect.

When beginning your exploration of this book, you'll achieve the best results if you approach it with a curious mind and open heart. Be sure you have a journal to take notes, and proceed slowly. Take time to linger over exercises and re-read sections that capture your interest. There is nothing to be gained by speed-reading the book from start to finish without taking the time necessary to integrate the practices and absorb the relevant material.

Peruse chapters 10, 11, and 12 to become familiar with the healing deities from various cultures before diving into chapters 1 through 9. Alternatively, you can begin to familiarize yourself with these divine healing helpers at any point as you progress through the materials.

It is my intention that these pages add to your healing toolkit, providing additional resources toward greater health and a more joyful life.

Chapter 1

Introduction to Your Divine Support System

When we incarnate into this world, we are assigned a team of spirit guides to assist us as we navigate our life's journey, both the wonderful and joyful times as well as the more challenging experiences. Some guides are with us for our entire lifetime. Others come to lend assistance during specific events or life stages. You may not be aware of these powerful allies, but that doesn't mean they haven't been with you, providing you with daily guidance, support, and encouragement since the moment of your birth.

When you embarked on your healing journey, new guides joined what I like to call your Divine Support System. Your relationship is best described as an alliance since it implies a mutual affinity for a particular outcome—specifically, an interest in your own healing and the healing of others. You have the ability to grow your spiritual healing team to include additional guides, angels, deities, and more. You control who is a member of your Divine Support System and can collaborate with these spiritual beings for greater health and happiness.

Although these divine beings don't have physical bodies or exist in the physical world as humans do, they do exist in the spiritual realms and are accessible to us. Many religious systems, cosmologies, and theories of the universe's origins revolve around these unseen realms and alternate planes of reality. Regardless of your personal belief system or religious background, you can interact with divine beings who can assist you with your healing endeavors.

There is a veil or border between our physical world and the realm of spirits. By crossing the border or peering through the veil, we can interact and form relationships with our spiritual allies on the other side. Many ancient texts such as the Bible, the Mahabharata, and the Book of Enoch, in addition to the myths and legends of cultures around the world and through time, describe how the spiritual realms interact with our physical plane. In modern times, numerous people channel messages from angels, and beings known as Ascended Masters bring messages across the veil. Opening yourself to these unseen realms allows you to participate in an ancient and powerful source of divine guidance and wisdom.

Setting Your Intention

Where do we begin our adventure of connecting with our Divine Support System? We start with creating our Divine Support System intention. Setting intentions is a powerful practice that can direct energy to produce a particular result and provides a structure or framework that can guide our choices and focus our thoughts and actions.

Imagine being in a boat on the ocean without a motor or a paddle. The ship would float aimlessly and be easily swept along by a current to an unpleasant or unwanted location. In this metaphor, your carefully crafted intention would be a paddle or motor, able to direct you on your life path and steer you toward your goal. Setting an intention is a simple, proactive step to keep yourself on target.

Let's begin by developing your intention to connect with your Divine Support System. First, set the stage for your intention-setting practice. Find a quiet location where you won't be disturbed. Silence your cell phone. You may want to light a candle or burn incense to create an atmosphere of sacred space for your experience.

Next, center yourself by taking long, deep breaths. An excellent breathing technique for focusing the mind is cultivating an equal breath by inhaling and exhaling for a specific amount of time—for example, inhaling for a count of four and exhaling for a count of four. Spend a few minutes focusing on your breath to clear your mind before continuing the intention-setting process.

Once your breathing is even and your mind settled, explore the parts of your life you wish to heal. Here are some suggestions to start the process:

- Physical healing for injuries, metabolism problems, immune disorders, sexual issues, fertility problems, illness, chronic conditions, disease, etc.
- Emotional healing for afflictions such as anger issues, eating disorders, depression, childhood trauma, grief, low self-esteem, etc.
- Mental healing for issues such as anxiety, stress, memory difficulties, learning disabilities, ADHD, etc.
- Spiritual healing for issues related to loss of faith, loss of purpose, and disconnection from the Divine/Source/God/ Goddess/the Creator
- Financial healing for difficulties related to loss of income, uncontrollable spending, budgeting issues, and inadequate housing
- Relationship healing for problems related to your connection with family members, children, friends, colleagues, or your significant other
- Ancestral healing for problems related to family patterns of abuse, financial lack, addiction, and inherited negative thought patterns

Also, consider elements of your life that are unhealthy or not in alignment with the version of yourself that you wish to become. First, examine your behavior patterns: Are there habits you want to eliminate, such as smoking, overindulging in food or drink, negative self-talk, or a social media obsession? Consider what changes you could make to increase your health, wellness, and overall happiness. For example, consider dedicating more time to your self-care, starting an exercise routine, examining your nutritional needs, learning stress reduction techniques, or engaging in more activities that bring you joy. Your Divine Support System can assist you with making these lifestyle changes.

If you are an energy worker or a medical professional, you can connect with your Divine Support System to become a more proficient healer. Consider these additional topics based on your unique needs and goals:

- Establishing healthy boundaries
- Increasing your knowledge of healing modalities
- Utilizing plants and crystals to heal others
- Establishing a self-care routine
- Improving your vitality and energy levels so you can continue to serve your community

To assist with developing your Divine Support System intention, list your goals, desires, and dreams for your connection to your Divine Support System. Consider all elements of yourself that need healing and write these aspirations in your journal.

Based on your unique goals and objectives, design your Divine Support System intention statement. Then, for best results, refer to this statement often as a reminder of why you've begun this journey toward greater health and happiness, in addition to your goals for cultivating relationships with your guides and deities.

Sample Divine Support System Intention Statement

I, (your name here), wish to develop relationships with my guides, angels, ancestors, and deities to assist me along my life path and for the specific purpose of [a summary of your goals]. Therefore, I will say *yes* to activities, choices, and thoughts that align with my goals of learning the tools and techniques to connect with these powerful energies and, in the process, improve my life physically, emotionally, mentally, and spiritually.

Today, with a grateful heart for my unique journey, I am ready to commit myself to cultivating relationships with my spirit guides, angels, ancestors, and deities, forming my personal Divine Support System.

Signed: _____

Date: _____

———————◆———————

Compose your Divine Support System intention statement in your journal.

Chapter 2

Collaborate with Your Divine Support System

Before meeting your Divine Support System, exploring some essential practices and skills is important. By developing your proficiency in these areas, you'll set the stage for successfully developing relationships with your guides and other beings of light who can assist you in achieving greater health and happiness.

Grounding

Grounding is a crucial practice as we delve into connecting with our Divine Support System. As the capacity to connect with the vibration of the earth, grounding connects us to our physical body, roots us in the present moment, enhances our ability to focus, provides us with stability, and assists us with establishing healthy boundaries. When we are aligned with the earth element and firmly grounded, we can more easily connect with our spirit allies.

Benefits connected with implementing a consistent grounding practice may include the following:

- Increase in focus, inner strength, and adaptability
- Decrease levels of stress, worry, and anxiety
- Greater connection to your physical body
- Enhanced mind-body-spirit connection

To deepen your connection to the energies of Mother Earth, I suggest developing your unique grounding toolkit. Experiment to see what practices and techniques resonate with you. For instance, you may find that taking a hike or spending time at the beach is the most effective practice to ground yourself. Or perhaps you prefer to use affirmations, positive statements that are repeated to generate a specific outcome. Here are suggestions to get you started as you develop your own grounding toolkit.

Activities

- Set up and care for a kitchen garden
- Spend time in nature gardening, walking, swimming, or hiking
- Connect with your pet (or a friend's pet)
- Recline in savasana (corpse pose) outside or inside, feeling a connection to the earth's grounding energy
- Receive a massage

Meditations

- Meditate outside while sitting on a rock or with your back against a tree
- Visualize the colors associated with the earth element in your meditation sessions: green and brown
- While meditating, imagine roots growing from your tailbone, journeying down your legs through your feet, and descending to the core of the earth, where your roots may pull up its grounding energy
- Experiment with meditating using the Prithvi mudra, a hand gesture known to provide a grounded state of being. With both hands, touch the tip of your ring finger to the tip of your thumb. Palms may be positioned upward to receive energy or downward for additional grounding.

Affirmations

- "I easily access the grounding energies of Mother Earth."
- "I exist in harmony and balance with the grounding vibration of the earth."

Various metaphysical tools can assist you in achieving a grounded state. You can experiment with meditating with crystals or placing crystals around your home. Crystals such as smoky quartz, hematite, chiastolite, and garnet can assist with grounding. Alternatively, essential oils such as vetiver, cedarwood, pine, spikenard, and sweet marjoram provide a sense of grounding. Essential oils can be used in a diffuser or applied topically. If applying directly to your skin, always use a carrier oil (like jojoba) to reduce the chance of skin irritation.

Grounding should be performed before connecting with your Divine Support System to ensure a stable connection to your spirit allies and a more dynamic flow of information.

Energy Clearing

Energy clearing involves the removal of negative or stagnant energy. The practice of energy clearing can be performed on yourself, your home, your office, and anywhere that energy can accumulate. Energy clearing can be done anytime, but it is a crucial step before connecting with your Divine Support System. There are many benefits to consistently using energy clearing techniques, including removing negative thought forms and emotions as well as raising your personal vibration and energy levels. The following energy clearing techniques cover a range of activities, from visualization to metaphysical tools.

Violet Flame Bathing

You only need your creative imagination for this visualization. Set your intention to clear yourself or a room of any negative and stagnant energies that may be present. Imagine a bright, vibrant violet flame at your heart center. Take a few deep breaths and visualize the flame becoming brighter. Now, the violet flame divides into two flames. Allow the two flames to travel from your heart center down both arms and into the palms of each hand. Each palm will now have a violet flame at its center. Proceed to bathe yourself in this violet light, using your hands as if washing yourself. Maintain this bathing visualization for a few minutes or until you feel a shift in your energy. When you are finished, imagine the violet flame retracting into your palms and traveling up both arms back into your heart center. Release the visualization. This practice can be modified to cleanse a room or another person.

Selenite Crystals

Selenite is a type of gypsum that has a milky white appearance. As a very high vibrational crystal, selenite can assist with the removal of negative and stagnant energy by raising the vibration of an individual or a room. To clear energy using a selenite crystal, sweep yourself or a space by holding the selenite crystal and steadily directing the crystal up and down.

Himalayan or Tibetan Singing Bowls

Singing bowls are a vibrational tool sound healers often use. When struck with a mallet or played in another way, these bowls produce unique tones that can create a relaxed, meditative state and also clear negative or stale energies. To begin energy clearing using singing bowls, simply set your intention to cleanse yourself of any negative energies that may be present. Then, holding the singing bowl in your palm, mindfully tap the rim or side of the bowl with a mallet. Pause as the sound bowl's vibrations surround you and your environment. You can repeat this process until you feel your energy shift. Another option is to circle the bowl's rim with the mallet, which produces a different tone and vibration.

Essential Oils

Essential oils are tools gifted to us by the plant kingdom. Wide varieties of essential oils can assist with the removal of lower vibrational and stagnant energies. A diffuser can transmit the essential oil throughout a room, or essential oils can be applied directly to the skin. However, if you plan to use an essential oil topically, use a carrier oil, such as jojoba, to reduce the chance of skin irritation. Experiment with jasmine, neroli, frankincense, lemongrass, cypress, and rosemary.

Support Skills for This Journey

As you prepare to meet your team of spiritual allies who can assist you with healing, consider what skills may assist you in this endeavor. Our spiritual guides don't have physical bodies; we can't converse with them by phone or email. As a result, specific skills can be cultivated and strengthened to make communication easier.

Quieting the Mind

Our minds are active and dynamic, skipping from one thought to another. Although this constant stream of thoughts assists us with our day-to-day lives, settling your mind to focus on connecting with your Divine Support System may be challenging. As a result, spending time quieting your mind is a valuable practice. When our minds are settled and calm, we are more open to receiving guidance and insights from both our own inner wisdom and the Divine.

Developing a consistent meditation practice is a crucial tool in quieting a restless mind. The essential component of meditation is to focus on an object and, as your mind wanders, gently return your awareness to the object of your meditation repeatedly. Start with a five-minute meditation, slowly increasing to twenty or thirty minutes. Training your mind to focus enables you to connect with your Divine Support System members more easily.

Your meditation practice can be as unique as you are. Some suggested meditation techniques may be found here, but you can experiment with additional ones.

- Take a walk outside, focusing on your physical body—the movement of your feet on the ground or your legs

- Seated outdoor meditation: Sit outdoors, close your eyes, and focus your attention on your ears and the sounds you hear
- Indoor meditation: Take a comfortable seat, close your eyes, and turn your attention to your breath, focusing on the inhale, the slight pause after the inhale, the exhale, and the brief pause after the exhale

Dynamic Imagination

Our imagination is a gift available to all of us. Your connection to your imagination may be strong, or perhaps you are less engaged with this aspect of yourself. Nevertheless, your imagination can play a vital role in developing your connection to your Divine Spirit Allies and your healing journey, including the following:

- Imagine the appearance of your spirit guides, ancestors, and other healing deities
- Imagine a place of healing, such as a garden or temple, where you can meet with your guides and other members of your divine healing team
- Imagine yourself being restored to perfect health

Visualizing and forming pictures in your mind's eye is a significant component of your imagination. Although visualization may not come quickly to you at first, it is a skill that can evolve over time with practice and patience.

Consider the following activities designed to help you develop your visualization skills and a dynamic imagination:

- Spend ten to fifteen minutes a day daydreaming
- Look at a picture of a statue, flower, painting, or building, and then recreate the image in your mind's eye as accurately as possible
- Create an affirmation such as "I embrace my creative, dynamic imagination and easily visualize images in my mind's eye"

Self-Knowledge

"Know Thyself" is an inscription found at the temple of Apollo at Delphi.[1] It's an invitation to understand our authentic selves. We are often so conditioned by our families, significant others, co-workers, friends, and society that we do not understand our true nature. As you begin your journey to meet your Divine Support System, take time for personal reflection. By understanding your preferences and your inclinations, apart from the norms of your home and society, you can achieve a closer relationship with your Divine Support System.

Consider the following questions and record your responses in your healing journal. These responses are your own private musings, so please answer honestly and without judgment after a period of reflection.

- What role does imagination play in your life?
- What are your feelings concerning unseen realms?
- Are you comfortable exploring other cultures?
- What are your views regarding angels?
- What role does intuition play in your life?
- Would you feel comfortable working with saints or deities of a different religion than yours?
- What are your thoughts regarding psychic senses such as clairvoyance?

Once you have completed this text, revisit these questions to see if your responses have changed.

Intuition

Your intuition is your gut reaction. Although we have access to our intuition, many individuals have disconnected from this remarkable ability, due in part to our society's focus on the rational mind and logical

---

1. Mark Morford, Robert J. Lenardon, Michael Sham, *Classical Mythology* (New York: Oxford University Press, 1986), 263.

thought. However, once we begin to tune into the subtle signals of our intuition, we can access the wealth that is intuitive guidance.

As you embark on this journey to form meaningful connections with your Divine Support System, consider the role your intuition can play. Intuition can provide insights as to which guides, ancestors, deities, and angels would be valued members of your healing team. It can also assist in determining the best method for connecting with your guides and crafting petitions or prayers for healing. Allow your intuition to help you along your path to greater overall health, giving you gentle nudges about your next best step toward greater well-being.

While strengthening your connection to your intuition, there are a few key things to keep in mind:

Listen to your gut response. The best way to develop and strengthen your intuition is to begin to trust your inner wisdom. Take a chance and listen to your gut.

Make journaling a habit. Start journaling your thoughts, feelings, and instincts. If doodling or drawing feels more natural, do it in your journal. When you understand yourself better, you can more easily tap into your intuitive nature.

Try dream journaling. Start documenting your dreams, including how you felt when you first woke up. Many intuitive insights can be found within our dreams, and dream journals are an excellent means of examining these messages from the dream world.

Certain crystals and essential oils are believed to assist with intuition development. Crystals such as sodalite, labradorite, and lapis lazuli can be used during meditation or around your home to awaken and strengthen your connection to your intuition. Additionally, you can diffuse or apply essential oils such as clary sage, Roman chamomile, frankincense, or lavender. If applying directly to your skin, use a carrier oil (like jojoba or sweet almond) to reduce the chance of skin irritation.

Relaxation

Modern living has its benefits but also carries the potential for chronic stress and anxiety. These states of mind make it difficult (if not impossible) to tap into your intuition, experience your psychic senses, and receive messages from your Divine Support System. Dedicating time each day to cultivate relaxation can benefit you in numerous ways, such as improving concentration, elevating your mood, improving sleep quality, lowering blood pressure, enhancing creativity, improving digestion, reducing stress hormones, and increasing energy levels and vitality.

The key to successful relaxation is self-awareness. Once you notice where tension exists, you know where to focus your energy to help alleviate or eliminate stress. A full-body scan is a simple practice to identify where you are holding tension and stress. Simply close your eyes and bring your attention to the top of your head. Then, slowly bring your awareness down to your face, relaxing and releasing the muscles in your face. Proceed to shift your attention gradually down your entire body. Notice any areas of tension and consciously relax those muscles. This process can be performed quickly in a few minutes or stretched out for fifteen minutes based on your needs and time constraints. To be most effective, perform the full body scan at least once daily.

Other practices that may assist with obtaining a state of relaxation are found here. Of course, everyone is different, so feel free to experiment to see which relaxation technique works best for you.

- Meditation
- Yoga Nidra
- Massage
- Acupuncture
- Reiki healing

- Spending time in nature
- Soaking in a bath
- Using a sauna
- Spending time with your pet or with animals

Crystals and essential oils are known for enhancing the relaxation process. You can experiment with meditating with crystals or placing crystals around your home. Crystals such as rose quartz, lepidolite, and kunzite can promote peace and tranquility within yourself and your environment. Moreover, essential oils such as lavender, ylang-ylang, bergamot, and jasmine relieve stress and enhance relaxation. Essential oils can be used in a diffuser or applied topically. If applying directly to your skin, use a carrier oil (like jojoba or sweet almond) to reduce the chance of skin irritation.

Chapter 3

Psychic Senses: Receiving Messages from Your Divine Support System

As you consciously begin to quiet your mind, actively use your imagination, and listen to your intuition, you may experience an awakening of your psychic senses. Psychic senses are also known as the "clair" senses, *clair* being French for "clear." These senses are phenomena arising from our intuition. Here is a description of eight psychic senses.

> *Clairvoyance or Clear-seeing:* Corresponds to the sense of sight and is the capacity to perceive through a "second sight," which may manifest as visions in the mind's eye or could be experienced as external vision through the physical eyes.

> *Clairaudience or Clear-hearing:* Corresponds to the sense of hearing and may be experienced as "inner hearing" or as sounds without a physical cause heard with the ears.

> *Claircognizance or Clear-knowing:* Corresponds to the sense of thinking and is the aptitude to receive a transfer of information instantly into the consciousness without any known source of information.

Clairtangency or Clear-touching: Corresponds to the sense of touch and is the aptitude for receiving previously unknown information by physically touching a person or object.

Clairempathy or Clear-feeling: The capacity to feel the emotions of another as if those emotions are your own.

Clairsentience or Clear-sensing: The aptitude to perceive an individual's energy or the vibe of a building, space, or object.

Clairgustance or Clear-tasting: Corresponds to our sense of taste and is the ability to perceive the flavor of something that is not in the mouth.

Clairalience or Clear-smelling: Corresponds to the sense of smell and is the ability to detect the odor or aroma of an object not physically present.

You may be naturally inclined toward exploring one or two of these psychic senses, but be receptive to receiving messages from your Divine Support System through all your clair- senses.

Clairvoyance and Your Divine Support System

Clairvoyance is one of the most well-known psychic senses. Clairvoyance can occur with physical sight—for example, seeing a person or object manifest that doesn't exist in the material plane. The person or object often appears translucent to less solid than other objects in the environment and may disappear immediately or diffuse slowly over a period of time. Another way clairvoyance can occur physically is by seeing signs in the environment, such as repeating numbers, unusual animals in out-of-the-ordinary places, and reoccurring messages on posters or advertisements.

Alternatively, clairvoyance can occur via the mind's eye as a vision or sequence of images that are often dynamic and have a tangible quality. During these clairvoyant visions, you may feel like you are actually in the scene. Clairvoyance can also be experienced in vivid dreams and daydreams containing intuitive messages, signs, and symbols. Individuals who prefer learning through visual methods and those who can visualize easily may have a natural affinity for clairvoyance.

Some ways you may experience clairvoyant messages or interactions with your Divine Support System include:

- Seeing spheres of light or orbs
- Seeing repeating animals, feathers, or other omens in your surroundings
- Experiencing vivid or prophetic dreams that may or may not feature a member of your Divine Support System
- Seeing repeating numbers such as on a clock, a sign, or a license plate
- Experiencing a vivid daydream featuring a member of your Divine Support System

Here are a couple of methods to develop your clairvoyant abilities.

Visualization: Practice your visualization techniques by creating uncomplicated images in your mind's eye, such as simple geometric shapes like a square or a triangle. Once you have mastered visualizing basic forms, try picturing a flower, including all the details. From there, try to recreate temples, statues, and landscapes. You strengthen your clairvoyant sense by focusing your awareness on your ability to visualize.

Affirmation: Design an affirmation that appeals to you, describing your future clairvoyant ability, such as "I see clearly through my inner sight and welcome the profound insights I receive." Repeat the affirmation often to receive the benefits.

Clairaudience and Your Divine Support System

Clairaudience is related to hearing, either with your physical ears or as internal messages. Something heard with your clairaudient physic sense does not have a physical origin. Individuals who prefer learning through auditory methods may have a natural affinity for clairaudience.

Some ways you may experience clairaudient messages or interactions with your Divine Support System may be found here:

- Receiving guidance, insights, and messages through what feels like a sense of inner hearing
- Hearing footsteps or doors closing or opening when no one is there
- Hearing unexplained whispers, murmurs, humming, or similar human noises
- Hearing voices in your head that aren't your own inner dialog
- Hearing music or musical instruments even though none are playing
- Hearing unexplained animal sounds such as chirping, barking, or purring

Here are a couple of methods to expand your clairaudient abilities:

Deep Listening: Our ears constantly provide us with information, but we aren't listening. Spend time each day with your eyes closed and open yourself up to listening to all the sounds in your environment. Start by listening to the sound of your breath and body. Slowly expand your awareness of sounds within a few feet of you until you are entirely open to receiving all auditory information. When you focus on your ability to hear, you connect with your clairaudient sense.

Affirmation: Craft an affirmation that resonates with you to facilitate the development of your clairaudient ability, such as "Sage wisdom and valuable insights are received easily through my inner ears." Recite your affirmation frequently to experience the benefits.

Please note that if you struggle with hearing voices that are not attributable to spirit guides or who give you messages that you believe are scary or harmful, seek the assistance of a mental health professional.

Claircognizance and Your Divine Support System

Claircognizance corresponds to knowing, and it may be described as a download of knowledge straight into your brain without an external source of information. You may have a natural gift for claircognizance if you have an active mind and enjoy activities such as reading and writing.

There are various ways you could experience claircognizant messages or interactions with your Divine Support System; here are a few:

- Knowing the right choice to make and what the result of making that decision will be
- Knowing the best resolution for a problem without any external or relevant information
- Knowing not to trust someone even though the person appears friendly and trustworthy
- Knowing when someone isn't telling the truth
- Knowing you must change your commute to work and, as a result, avoid a significant traffic accident
- Knowing which members to add to your Divine Support System and how they can assist you along your healing path

Explore different methods to strengthen your claircognizant abilities. Consider the following:

Lie Detector Practice: This exercise requires a friend or family member. Close your eyes and have a friend or family member tell you something true. Notice if your mind knows that it's the truth. Now, have your friend or family member tell you something untrue. Notice if you can tell the difference. Next, have your friend or family member tell you a series of truths and lies that would be previously unknown to you. After each statement, write down whether it's true or false. Afterward, discuss your results to see how accurate your impressions were. Keep practicing with different friends, family members, or even acquaintances to develop your claircognizance abilities. By focusing your attention on the workings of your mind, you are strengthening your claircognizance psychic sense.

Affirmation: Design an affirmation that connects with you regarding developing your claircognizance ability, such as "My mind is receptive to the insights and wisdom of the cosmos." Repeat the affirmation often to receive the benefits.

Clairtangency and Your Divine Support System

Clairtangency corresponds to the psychic sense of touch that occurs when an individual receives previously unknown information by physically touching an object, person, or animal. An example of clairtangency is handling an object and receiving an impression about its history. Individuals inclined toward experiencing clairtangency typically have a highly developed sense of touch and may have very sensitive skin.

If you are naturally inclined toward clairtangency, here are some ways you might experience interactions with your Divine Support System:

- Experiencing a deep connection to an ancestor while handling an object the individual previously owned
- While touching crystals, essential oils, or plants, experiencing knowledge of their healing properties
- While touching people or animals, experiencing an inner knowing or feeling about their health or mood

You can develop your clairtangent abilities in various ways, including the following:

Antique Store Exercise: Go to an antique store, thrift store, yard sale, or use any found item. Find an object that sparks your curiosity, such as a piece of furniture, a dish, or a figurine. Take a few deep breaths and notice how you feel physically, mentally, and emotionally. Then, bring your awareness to your chosen object and place your hand on it. Relax your mind and open yourself to receive any impressions about the object's history, such as previous owners. This information may come to you as a picture in your mind's eye, a feeling, an auditory response, or a simple knowing. Try various other objects and compare the results. When you focus on the impressions you receive when touching things and people, your clairtangent ability will develop and strengthen.

Affirmation: Compose an affirmation centered on developing your clairtangency, for example, "I easily receive information and insights by touching people and objects." Repeat the affirmation often to receive the benefits.

Clairempathy and Your Divine Support System

Clairempathy corresponds to our ability to relate to the emotions of another. Clairempathy may present itself as feeling another person's emotions as if they were your own. Although it may be valuable to connect deeply with the emotions of another, it can be challenging to separate yourself from these extreme feelings. The energy-clearing techniques found in chapter 2 may help if the emotions perceived through your clairempathic senses become overwhelming or unwelcome.

If you are naturally inclined toward clairempathy, here are some ways you might experience interactions with your Divine Support System.

- Experience supportive and comforting emotions as your Divine Support System connects with you through your emotional body
- Experience support establishing and maintaining your boundaries, which is a challenge for those with clairempathy
- Experience divine assistance recharging and replenishing your energy

There are many ways to develop your clairempathic abilities. Here are a couple:

Emotional Awareness: Spend time in an environment where you can observe others, such as sitting in a park or shopping center. Pick out one person and sense their feelings: joyful, sad, delighted, under the weather, anxious. Try to feel these emotions within your own body. Once you have attempted this practice, clear yourself energetically by taking a few deep breaths and picture yourself surrounded by white light. Then, repeat the exercise a few more times. When you focus your attention on the emotions of others and your responses to those emotions, you strengthen your clairempathic psychic sense.

Affirmation: Develop an affirmation that connects with you regarding developing your clairempathy physic sense, such as "I am intimately attuned with the emotional landscapes of others." Repeat the affirmation often to receive the benefits.

Clairsentience and Your Divine Support System

Clairsentience is the ability to perceive another individual's energy or the "vibe" of a place or object. For example, the energy of crowds of people may feel overwhelming, and the energy of physical surroundings easily influences the naturally clairsentient.

If you are predisposed toward clairsentience, here you'll find some ways you might experience interactions with your Divine Support System.

- Receiving information through the energy of crystals and plants for healing and personal growth
- Receiving divine support while navigating the energetic frequencies of large crowds
- Receiving divine assistance in trusting the information you receive through your clairsentient psychic sense and taking the appropriate action

There are many ways to develop your clairsentient abilities, including these examples:

Stone or Crystal Exercise: Select a crystal or stone (a stone from your backyard is perfectly acceptable). Take a comfortable seat and begin to focus on your stone. Using the infinity loop method, send your awareness to the stone and invite the stone's energy back to you as if the energy exchange takes the shape of an infinity loop. Open yourself up to receive information about the stone's origins, history, and how you might use its energy for healing. Record any insights you might receive in your journal. When you focus your attention on the "vibe" or energy of a person, place, or object, you strengthen your clairsentient ability.

Affirmation: Craft an affirmation focusing on developing your clairsentient psychic sense, such as "I can effortlessly receive and interpret the 'vibes' of people, places, and things." Recite the affirmation frequently to receive the benefits.

Clairgustance and Your Divine Support System

Clairgustance is your psychic sense of taste and takes place when you have a taste in your mouth without a physical cause. Typical tastes associated with clairgustance include metal, chemicals, blood, and even cigarettes, in addition to food and drink. Typically, those inclined toward experiencing clairgustance have a highly developed sense of taste.

Here are some ways you might experience interactions with your Divine Support System if you are clairgustant:

- Experiencing known or unknown tastes in your mouth when communicating with your Divine Support System that may trigger specific feelings or intuitive guidance
- Experiencing intuitive knowledge and guidance while eating or drinking
- Experiencing an unusual taste in your mouth when you are ill or near someone who is unwell
- Experiencing an unexplained taste in my mouth when thinking about an ancestor or divine spirit helper

There are many ways to strengthen your clairgustant abilities, including the following:

Conscious Tasting Practice: Select a flavorful item to engage with your sense of taste, such as a piece of high-quality chocolate or a portion of fruit. With your eyes closed, notice how you feel physically, mentally, and emotionally. Take a few cleansing breaths, then place the item in your mouth. Pause and observe the sensation of it in your mouth. Slowly begin to chew and notice as the flavor releases. Pause and perceive if you feel any changes in your physical, mental, or emotional bodies. Place another piece of your selected food in your mouth and mindfully begin to chew with your complete awareness of the food's taste. After swallowing, pause and notice if any memories or other intuitive guidance appear. Repeat often with various types of food and compare your results. When you focus your awareness on your ability to taste, you'll enhance your clairgustant ability.

Affirmation: Compose an affirmation to strengthen your
   clairgustance, such as "I have a highly developed sense of
   taste and effortlessly receive intuitive guidance through
   my clairgustance psychic sense." Repeat your affirmation
   regularly to receive the best results.

Clairalience and Your Divine Support System

Clairalience is associated with our sense of smell and intimately connected to our feelings and memories. Clairalience occurs when you detect an aroma with your physical nose but the source is not present in
your physical environment. Alternatively, your brain may identify a scent
even though the source of the smell isn't present. Typical smells associated with the psychic sense of clairalience are flowers, grass, smoke, cigarettes, food, decomposition, cologne or perfume, and the smell of the
ocean. Those predisposed to clairalience typically have a highly developed sense of smell.

If you are naturally inclined toward clairalience, here are some ways
you might experience interactions with your Divine Support System.

- Experiencing known or unknown aromas when
   communicating with your Divine Support System may
   trigger emotional responses, memories, or intuitive guidance
- Experiencing intuitive knowledge and guidance while using
   essential oils and incense
- Experiencing unusual and unpleasant scents when you are ill
   or when you are near someone who is unwell

Experiment with various ways to strengthen your clairalient physic
sense, including the following:

Conscious Smelling Exercise: Select something aromatic, such
   as essential oils or flowers (another excellent option is
   freshly ground coffee). With your eyes closed, notice how
   you feel physically, mentally, and emotionally. Take a few

cleansing breaths and then inhale deeply the scent of your selected item. Pause and observe if you feel any changes in your physical, mental, or emotional bodies. Take another deep breath of the same aroma. Pause and notice if any memories surface or intuitive guidance is received. Repeat with various scented objects and compare your results. You connect with and strengthen your clairalient psychic sense by focusing your awareness on your ability to smell.

Affirmation: Compose an affirmation with the aim of developing your clairalience physic sense, such as: "I am strongly connected to my sense of smell, easily receiving intuitive guidance through my clairalience psychic sense." Recite your affirmation frequently to receive the best results.

Now that we have established a strong foundation of practice, we are ready to explore the types of spirit team members that may comprise your healing alliance.

Chapter 4
Types of Spirit Healing Allies

When it comes to what sorts of spirit healing allies can be included in your Divine Support System, the options are unlimited. You can draw inspiration from modern or ancient religions, myths, your family tree, or even nature. You are only limited by your imagination.

Personal Spirit Guides

These beings of divine origin are tasked with assisting you along your life path. Spirit guides exist in the cosmic realm as beings of light or energy and are unique to you. They are able to act as mentors, advisors, and teachers. Some of your spirit guides will be with you for your entire lifetime, while others may assist you with a specific challenge or significant life event. Although you have a personal spirit guide dedicated to assisting you in your day-to-day life, you can call upon specialized guides to help with specific areas of interest. Some suggestions regarding health, healing, happiness, and overall well-being may be found below:

- Healer spirit guides assist you with your personal healing journey, finding the most appropriate doctors, the most effective healing practices, and the best treatments
- Teacher spirit guides provide knowledge, wisdom, and insights on various topics, including healing, health care, and overall well-being

- Protector spirit guides act as guardians, protecting your physical body, guarding your health, and providing direction regarding your personal safety
- Joy spirit guides provide advice on cultivating more joy and happiness in daily life, which contributes to your overall well-being. They can also assist with issues concerning depression.
- Creative spirit guides assist with developing innovative healing solutions to problems and enhancing creativity
- Vitality spirit guides assist with cultivating powerful and active energy as well as the strength to combat disease and illness
- Spirit guides of a specific healing lineage can assist with developing the tools and techniques of a particular healing lineage, such as Reiki

Ancestors

When we speak of ancestors, we refer to those individuals who no longer live with us on this plane of existence. Ancestors were once humans who walked the earth and had a connection to us. Although we may think of ancestors as only those we are directly connected to by genetics, the realm of the ancestors is vast, and the possibilities for connection are endless. Here are categories of the types of ancestors you may consider adding to your Divine Support System.

Blood Ancestors

These are the ancestors you are directly related to through your DNA, consisting of your parents, grandparents, and great-grandparents all the way back to the first father and first mother. Our ancestors by blood can prove to be a mixed bag when it comes to support; we may have family members who were challenging individuals. However, as we evolve and heal ourselves, our ancestors (even the challenging ones) may also benefit and receive healing. Activities such as creating a family tree can help us identify our blood ancestors and learn valuable information about our heritage in the process. Working with our blood ancestors as part of our Divine Support System can assist us with healing family traumas and negative patterns of behaviors passed down through the generations.

Ancestors through Adoption or Foster Care

If you were adopted or placed in foster care, you might not know your blood ancestors, and that's okay. You also have an intimate connection to your adopted or foster family and their lineage. When your adopted or foster family assumed responsibility for your care and protection, you became a part of their family and their legacy. Personal story: I am adopted and have successfully worked with both my blood and adopted ancestors. Remember that there is no right or wrong in this practice. Do what feels most natural to you based on your unique situation.

Ancestors of the Land

These powerful allies are the ancestors not directly related to you by blood or by raising you but those connected to you based on where you currently reside. These are the ancestors who once lived where you do now. Connection to these ancestors can be enhanced based on your ability to create a relationship with the land on which you live. Consider researching the history of your town and those individuals who inhabited the grounds before you. As potential members of your Divine Support System, ancestors of the land you live upon can provide safety and security in your home, a sense of grounding, reduced stress and anxiety, and overall well-being.

By Affinity

Your affinities, interests, and inclinations connect you to those who share them. Because a natural rapport exists, these ancestors can assist you. Types of affinity can include your profession, career, hobbies, and skills. For example, if you are a Reiki healer, one ancestor by affinity would be Dr. Mikao Usui, the founder of Reiki. As potential members of your Divine Support System, ancestors of affinity can assist with repairing work relationships, honing your skills, and removing blocks preventing you from advancement.

By Spiritual Lineage

These are the ancestors linked to us by our religion or spiritual practice. Even if you no longer practice the religion of your birth, you may still find allies for healing based on this religion. Ancestors of spiritual lineage can assist with all types of healing, in addition to any spiritual healing needed.

Ancestors from Past Lives

If past lives are part of your belief system, consider connecting with individuals you've had connections with during your previous incarnations. As part of your Divine Support System, these ancestors can assist with healing patterns of behavior associated with your past lives and irrational fears that don't appear to have a connection to your blood or adoptive ancestors. To help identify your past lives, consider connecting with them during meditation, hypnotherapy, or dreams.

Deities

A deity is a sacred being of divine origin gifted with powers beyond the scope of mortals. Deities are known to interact with humans, assisting them along their evolutionary and spiritual paths. Cultures around the world, from ancient times to the modern era, have turned to deities to assist with all aspects of life, including (but not limited to) health, abundance, good fortune, the process of dying, and the afterlife.

Religions are centered around worshiping a particular deity or a group of deities. Whether or not you choose to work within your current religious structure is your choice; however, the deities and other spiritual beings assembled in chapter 10 are accessible no matter your religious or ethnic background.

Angels and Archangels

Angles and archangels are divine beings of pure light. With two notable exceptions, the archangels Metatron and Sandalphon, angelic beings have never incarnated as humans. Instead, they can be best described as pure, divine, conscious energy. Angels have specific areas of expertise and act as intermediaries between humans and the Source/Creator/Supreme Being/God/Goddess. Angels are often depicted in human form with wings and a halo. However, they may also be envisioned as geometric patterns, orbs, or fields of colored light.

Ascended Masters

Ascended Masters are beings who were once human and, having achieved a state of enlightenment, dedicated their existence to the planet's spiritual evolution. Ascended Masters act as teachers of humanity and are now immortal due to their state of enlightenment. The theosophical teachings of the late 1800s reference Ascended Masters as Mahatmas, the Masters of Ancient Wisdom. Ascended Masters are all-inclusive and will work with anyone who contacts them for assistance. These powerful spiritual allies exist beyond the constraints of time and space. Although lists of Ascended Masters may vary according to their sources, Ascended Masters are renowned for their diligence in assisting humanity and providing inspiration, guidance, motivation, and insights for both spiritual evolution and healing.

Saints, Bodhisattvas, and Sages

Many religions, in addition to Catholicism, recognize saints as individuals who lived lives of dedication to a spiritual ideal and often faced extreme hardships during their lifetime. Saints can be viewed as emulating an aspect of God embodying a particular virtue. Saints can be called upon to assist with their area of expertise and are known to provide miraculous assistance to whoever requests help, regardless of religious affiliation.

In Buddhism, bodhisattvas are spiritually enlightened individuals who are driven by compassion to assist others with enlightenment. Although there are nuances in the definition of bodhisattvas between the various Buddhist traditions, bodhisattvas embody what are known together as the four divine abodes or four immeasurables: lovingkindness, compassion, empathetic joy, and equanimity. Bodhisattvas have achieved the Buddha mind and embody Buddha's compassion for every sentient being, like that of a mother for her child, for whom she would gladly sacrifice her own life if necessary. Bodhisattvas can be called upon to assist with all types of suffering and are a source of comfort and healing.

Sages are individuals who possessed great wisdom, discernment, and solid judgment during their lifetimes. Although they may not have been regarded for their spirituality, they made tremendous contributions to society. For example, the Swiss psychiatrist and psychoanalyst Carl Jung may be considered a sage in the field of mental health. Anne Sullivan, the American educator known for assisting Helen Keller, who could not see or hear, may be considered a sage for working with those facing the challenges of disabilities. Clara Harlowe Barton was an American nurse and founder of the American Red Cross who may be regarded as a sage related to physical healing. Sages can be called upon to provide guidance, inspiration, and healing for their particular area of expertise.

Elementals

Elementals can be described as the consciousness or spiritual essences of the elements: earth, water, air, and fire. The Swiss Renaissance physician and alchemist, Paracelsus, described the elements as beings corresponding to each of the four elements. Paracelsus did not categorize these beings as spirits per se but as beings occupying a place between humans and spirits.[2] He hypothesized that working with the four elements and elemental beings would positively affect one's physical, mental, and emotional well-being. The categories of the elemental spirit helpers are as follows:

---

2. Manly P. Hall, *Paracelsus, the Four Elements and Their Spirits: Esoterics Classics* (New Haven, CT: Lamp of Trismegistus, 2021), 15.

- Gnomes are the elementals associated with the earth element
- Undines are the elementals related to the water element
- Sylphs are the elementals associated with the air element
- Salamanders are the elementals related to the fire element

Crystal and Plant Allies

Crystals and plants have been used for healing purposes for millennia. They are gifts from Mother Nature. Like the elements, each crystal and plant has a consciousness and spiritual essence. These crystal and plant kingdom spirits can assist us with our healing endeavors. Crystal allies can help with the use of crystals and stones for healing, meditation, protection, and deepening our connection to the Divine. Plant allies can aid us in receiving the healing benefits from the plants we consume through our food, teas, and flower essences. Additionally, plant allies can provide healing through the presence of flowers and plants in our homes and gardens and through essential oils, which can either be diffused or applied directly to the skin.

Animal Spirit Helpers

Animal spirit helpers can be valuable healers, teachers, and protectors. In this context, animal spirit helpers are not the spirit of an individual animal—instead, they are the archetypal essence of that animal or an "over-spirit." Each animal spirit helper has its own talents and abilities. Although providing a complete listing is outside this book's scope, I recommend *Animal Spirit Guides: An Easy-to-Use Handbook for Identifying and Understanding Your Power Animals and Animal Spirit Helpers* by Steven D. Farmer (Hay House, 2006) for a useful reference. Here's a sample of the various animal spirit helpers, complete with a description of their healing attributes:

Bear: Bear spirit animal helpers are wonderful physical
and emotional healing allies. They can assist with setting
boundaries, including energetic boundaries. Additionally,
they can help you find the courage to face your fears.

Camel: Camel spirit animal helpers can provide support for financial healing as well as the stamina to meet your healing goals

Cow: Cow spirit animal helpers are terrific resources to assist with the healing of relationships. They can also help with nurturing yourself and receiving the benefits of nourishment—physically, emotionally, mentally, or spiritually.

Duck: Duck spirit animal helpers can assist with fertility issues, self-acceptance, and emotional healing. They are also excellent guides for inviting more fun and enjoyment into your life.

Ladybug: Ladybug spirit animal helpers are amazing allies who can aid with reducing fear, anxiety, and stress. They can also help with rekindling your zest for life and overall happiness.

Octopus: Octopus spirit animal helpers are exceptional partners whenever regeneration is needed, and you need recovery. They can also assist with physical, mental, and emotional flexibility.

The vast community of spirit allies is available for assistance with your health and healing goals. From ancient gods and goddesses to plant and animal spirit helpers, your choices in selecting your Divine Support System members are limitless. Now let's explore how to choose which spirit allies and healing guides might best assist you on your personal journey.

Chapter 5

Select the Members of Your Divine Support System

The choice of members in your Divine Support System is a personal one. However, as you begin deciding which healing allies to invite into your Divine Support System, there are some helpful suggestions and guidelines you may want to consider.

The Size of Your Divine Support System

Bigger isn't always better when it comes to your Divine Support System. Quality is more important than quantity. Although there is no limit to the number of spiritual helpers that can participate in your Divine Support System, focusing on forming relationships with one or two spiritual beings at first may provide better, more tangible results than calling in twenty or thirty spiritual helpers with whom you haven't yet established a relationship.

Consider the situation where you need assistance. Would you get better results calling your best friend(s) and asking for a favor, or calling a large group of acquaintances? Since you have an established relationship with your best friend or a small group of close friends, the odds are better that they will answer your call for help quickly and effectively. The same is true for the members of your Divine Support System.

Consciously form relationships with one or two spiritual allies and add new teammates to your Divine Support System over time to create deep, intimate connections that will aid you in all aspects of your healing journey. As you deepen and strengthen these relationships, your Divine Support System may grow to ten or fifteen treasured spirit allies ready to guide, protect, encourage, and heal you.

Personal Preferences

Self-knowledge is an essential aspect of personal growth and healing. Along with clearly understanding your motivations and goals for your healing journey, it's also important to be aware of your preferences, biases, and natural inclinations, especially when selecting your Divine Support System members. When performing this self-analysis, please do not judge yourself—be honest and accepting of your answers, whatever they may be.

In your journal, write down your responses to the questions in this section to assess the types of members you may want to include in your Divine Support System. Cultivating relationships with a particular divine being is a personal preference. Remember that there are no right or wrong answers.

> *Personal Spirit Guides:* What are my feelings related to personal spirit guides? Am I open to working with personal spirit guides for healing? If so, what type of spirit guides (healing, teacher, protector, etc.) might best assist me at this time in my life and why?

> *Ancestors:* What is my relationship with my ancestors? Am I interested in pursuing a relationship with my ancestors at this time for the purpose of healing? If so, what type of ancestors (blood, land, affinity, spiritual lineage, past lives) support my healing goals?

> *Deities:* What are my feelings regarding the topic of deities? Am I open to working with deities to achieve my greater

health and well-being goals? If so, am I interested in
only exploring the deities associated with my religion or
ethnicity, or am I interested in exploring the deities related
to other religions and cultures? If so, what cultures do I feel
an affinity toward?

Angels and Archangels: What is my view regarding angels? Do
I feel a connection to the angelic realms? Am I interested
in working with angels and archangels for the purpose of
healing at this time? Take a few moments to reflect on the
reason(s) for your responses.

Ascended Masters: What are my opinions regarding Ascended
Masters? Do I feel a connection to the mission of the
Ascended Masters, which is the world's spiritual evolution?
Am I interested in exploring my relationship with Ascended
Masters for assistance on my healing path? Pause and
contemplate the rationale for your answers.

Saints: What is my reaction to the term "saint?" What would
it feel like to work with saints for the purposes of healing?
Am I interested in establishing a relationship with a saint at
this time? Consider the reasons behind your attitude toward
working with saints.

Bodhisattvas: What are my feelings regarding Bodhisattvas?
Do I feel connected to their mission to reduce the suffering
of all sentient beings and assist with the process of
enlightenment? Am I interested in developing a personal
relationship with bodhisattvas for the purpose of healing?
Why or why not?

Sages: What is my response to the term "sage?" Could I see
myself forming relationships with individuals of great
wisdom or specific knowledge who may be of assistance

along my healing path? Consider the reasons for your responses.

Elementals: What is my understanding of the term "elemental?" Do I have any interest in learning more about the four elements of earth, water, air, and fire for the purposes of healing? Take a moment or two to contemplate the rationale for your answers.

Crystal Allies: Do I have an affinity for crystals? Am I interested in learning more about the healing energies and innate consciousness of crystals? Spend a moment to consider the reasons for your response.

Plant Allies: Am I drawn to plants and flowers? Am I interested in forming a deep connection with the healing energies of the plant kingdom? Consider the *why* behind your answers.

Animal Spirit Helpers: Do I have a connection to animals? Do I feel drawn to working with animal spirit helpers for the purpose of healing? If so, are there particular animals that are of interest? If so, why?

Periodically refer to your answers to see if your personal preferences shift as you work through this book and as you begin forming relationships with your Divine Support System. You might find yourself ready to step outside of your current comfort zone.

Method of Selecting Members of Your Divine Support System

You can explore many ways to select the members of your Divine Support System. You might find inspiration from the suggestions in this section or take a completely different approach. You have the autonomy and the power to determine what your criteria will be. Your Divine Support System reflects your personal preferences and will be unique to you.

Specialization of the Spirit Ally

You may choose to select members of your Divine Support System based on the specialization of the divine being. Some spirit beings specialize in healing from physical illness, trauma, relationship healing, emotional healing, and so on. Additionally, spirit allies can assist with protection and financial health. Some divine beings provide general healing assistance. If you have specific healing goals, research spirit allies who focus on that healing element.

Category of Spirit Helper

You may be drawn to working with a specific kind of healing ally based on the type of divine being. Refer to your healing journal regarding your personal preferences. Are you interested in pursuing a relationship with a particular type of spirit helper? If so, that might be where you start your selection process.

Intuition

Your intuition is a divine gift and can be helpful when selecting your Divine Support System members. Your intuition isn't governed by logical thought. When using your intuition to determine which spirit ally can best assist you in your healing journey, quiet your mind and set the intention to make the best intuitive selection. Review the categories of spirit helpers or the encyclopedia of spirit helpers beginning in chapter 10. When you have a gut reaction or an inner knowing that this divine being would be a special healing companion to you, listen to this guidance and add this spirit helper to your Divine Support System.

Spirit Ally Cards

When there are many spirit helpers you feel drawn toward working with, spirit ally cards may be a beneficial tool to assist in choosing the most appropriate guides for you. You'll need index cards or another form of blank square card stock. List the names of the divine beings you're considering adding to your Divine Support System. On each card, write the name of one spirit helper or draw an image of them if you are artistically inclined. Turn the cards over blank side up. Shuffle or mix up the cards and lay them on a table or flat surface. Set the intention to select a card (or cards) with the spirit helpers that will be the best guides for you now. Then, select the card or cards that you are most drawn toward. Finally, turn over the card(s) to reveal the newest member(s) of your Divine Support System.

Previous Relationship or Connection

A previous relationship or connection to a specific angel, deity, saint, or other divine being can be expanded and deepened by adding this divine being to your Divine Support System. Even if this link existed in your earlier childhood or your dreams, the relationship could be expanded and deepened by adding this spirit helper to your Divine Support System.

Bibliomancy

Bibliomancy is a form of divination that uses a book or sacred text to provide guidance or information about the future. To use bibliomancy to determine the members of your Divine Support System, flip to chapter 10. Close your eyes and set the intention to select the most helpful spirit allies for your healing journey. Then, select a random page from the appropriate section. With your eyes still closed, move your finger down the page until you feel the need to pause. The spiritual helper upon which your finger is resting is the selected member of your Divine Support System. If you use this method, reflect on why this particular spirit helper might suit you and record your impressions in your healing journal.

Astrology

Astrology is the ancient art of examining the movement of the planets and stars for both personal development and foretelling future events. You don't have to be a professional astrologer to use astrology to select members of your Divine Support System. The ways in which you can use astrology to improve health and well-being are limitless, but two powerful suggestions are provided here. One employs astrology to determine your elemental composition, and the second focuses on asteroids.

ASTROLOGY APPROACH ONE: THE ELEMENTS

Astrology can provide insights regarding our elemental makeup, showing where we may lack earth, water, air, or fire. Armed with this knowledge, we could thus add a member to our Divine Support System to assist us with strengthening and healing this aspect of ourselves. To determine your unique elemental composition, you could reference an ephemeris (a table of planetary positions at the time of your birth) or use astrological software. In addition, there are many websites that can calculate your information for you, astro.com being the most popular. After you determine the placements of the planets in your natal chart, look at the following chart to determine your elemental constitution and decide if there is an element that would benefit from healing. You can then focus on adding an angel, deity, or master to assist you with healing and strengthening that element.

Aries, Leo, and Sagittarius are associated with the fire element related to vitality, passion, personal power, self-confidence, willpower, and drive. Archangel Michael, fire/solar gods and goddesses, and fire elementals can assist with healing and strengthening the fire element.

Taurus, Virgo, and Capricorn are associated with the earth element related to the physical realm with a focus on financial health, responsibilities, grounding, sensuality, patience, survival needs, and the ability to manifest. Archangel Uriel, gods and goddess associated with the earth or nature, and earth elementals can aid in healing and strengthening the earth element.

Gemini, Libra, and Aquarius are associated with the air element related to mental health, intelligence, communication skills, social skills, curiosity, and tolerance. Archangel Raphael, air elementals, as well as gods and goddesses associated with the wind, communication, and knowledge, can provide healing of the air element.

Cancer, Scorpio, and Pisces are associated with the water element related to emotional health, intuition, the sub-conscious mind, relationships, compassion, empathy, psychic senses, the ability to nurture, and adaptability. Archangel Gabriel, water/oceanic/river gods and goddesses, and water elements can heal and strengthen this element.

ASTROLOGY APPROACH TWO: ASTEROIDS

Another option for using astrology to determine members of your Divine Support System is the use of asteroids. These small, rocky celestial bodies orbit the sun, and there are more than one million known asteroids in the universe. Many asteroids are given names of gods and goddesses, offering insight into these heavenly objects' characteristics and astrological significance.

When examining your birth chart, you can look for asteroids close to the seven traditional planets: the Sun, Moon, Mercury, Venus, Mars, Jupiter, and Saturn. The asteroid should be within a degree or two of a planet to have an effect. If you have an asteroid close to one of the traditional planets, you may have an affinity with its related god or goddess and can call upon them to join your Divine Support System.

There are two methods to find these asteroids. The most accessible is using astrological software that includes asteroids. Once again, astro .com provides the option to select specific asteroids, either by the name of the asteroid or by their associated number. Select "Horoscope" and "Extended Chart Selection." Enter your birth date as the calculation date and proceed to the bottom of the page, where you will be provided with the option under "Additional Object" to select asteroids by either name or number.

The second method is to use an asteroid ephemeris, which provides the position of asteroids at a given point in time. In addition to online ephemeris options is *The Ultimate Asteroid Book* by J. Lee Lehman (Red Feather, 1998), an excellent resource for the mythology of popular asteroids that contains an ephemeris.

Adding and Removing Members of Your Divine Support System

Although there is no special ceremony or ritual to add or remove your Divine Support System members, there are a few practices you can follow. Before adding a new member to your Divine Support System, it's important to familiarize yourself with the mythology associated with the spirit helper. Also, take time to identify how the spirit ally may assist you with your specific healing goals. Depending on what you've learned, consider engaging with a practice or activity to align with their energies. Write down your intention for adding this new member of your Divine Support System in your healing journal.

Once you've crafted your intention, call aloud upon the spirit helper as you would a close friend, asking them to join your Divine Support System. State why you would like this divine being in your circle of healing allies; describe your healing goals, as well as how you require assistance. When you have finished, thank the spirit ally for participating and guiding you toward greater health and happiness.

If the time comes when you feel the need to remove a member of your Divine Support System, you can start by documenting why you are removing a particular spirit helper in your healing journal. Write a letter of gratitude for the spirit ally's assistance on a separate piece of paper. When you are ready, call upon the spirit helper aloud. Then, read your letter of gratitude aloud to your spirit helper. State that you no longer need the assistance of this healing ally. If you wish, add language that the dismissal may not be permanent; you may call upon the split helper again if needed. Finally, release the power of your intention into the world, either by burying your letter of gratitude in the earth or safely burning it.

───────◆───────

Choosing your Divine Support System members is a powerful and exciting process that should be approached thoughtfully. Before proceeding to the next chapter, consider composing a list of potential Divine Support System members using whichever method resonates with you. Remember, you control which healing guides and spirit allies you include in your healing alliance.

Chapter 6
Meet Your Divine Support System

We are now ready to set the stage to formally begin working with your Divine Support System. As we approach this practice, we should consider the difference between invoking and inviting. When a spirit being is invoked, you are using your power to call the spirit being into your space; in a sense, you are forcing it to appear whether the being wishes to be there or not. Invocation is, therefore, not appropriate to use with your Divine Support System—instead, you are inviting your spirit allies to join you on your healing journey. It is an invitation, not a command. Since you are requesting the presence and assistance of these divine beings, there are recommended practices that will ensure a more successful outcome.

Creating Sacred Space

Creating a sacred place of healing to connect with your Divine Support System doesn't require hours of preparation or intricate rituals. When we develop a sacred healing space, we create a safe, secure, and tranquil environment suitable for communing with our Divine Support System and participating in our healing process. The sacred space should be clean and tidy, free of distractions. Be sure to turn off your cell phone when you are in it. You will need a chair or meditation cushion to sit on while connecting with your Divine Support System. You can add to the serene ambiance of your space by lighting candles, electric or traditional, if you like.

Above all, the most critical part of your sacred healing space is you and your devotion to your healing endeavors. From a place of peace and harmony, we can connect with and co-create alongside our Divine Support System.

EXERCISE
Creation of Sacred Space—
Divine White Light Method

1. Select the room you will use for your sacred space and silence your cell phone. Sit momentarily and experience the quality of the room's energy. Don't attach judgment to your impressions. Remain as objective as possible and record your observations in your healing journal. Note the room's energy: is it open, inviting, supportive, and energetically "clean," or is there a heaviness or oppressive energy?

2. Set a five-minute timer and take a comfortable seat. Close your eyes and picture yourself seated in the room. Expand your view to include the building in which you are located. Now, expand your view further to include the moon, sun, and planets until you are at the very edge of the solar system. Now visualize a spark of divine white light descending from the heavens. The divine spark grows bigger and brighter as it passes by the planets, the sun, and the moon. The divine spark is now a large sphere of brilliant white light slowly passing through the building where you live and saturating your sacred space with holy light.

3. Sit with this visualization until the end of the session. Take a few cleansing breaths. Notice the quality of the room's energy. Has the energy changed? In your healing journal, document

any thoughts, emotions, or physical sensations that might occur as you sit in your sacred space.

The Divine White Light method can be used anytime to create sacred space. However, it's not the only method. For example, you can also use the appropriate symbols to generate sacred space if you are a Reiki healer. The most important aspect of creating sacred space is your intention.

The Power of Scents: Incense and Essential Oils

Your sense of smell is one of the most potent in your possession. This sense, in particular, is strongly linked to memory and can stimulate an emotional response. You may choose to incorporate the use of either incense or essential oils as part of your practice when communicating with your Divine Support System. If you use the same incense or essential oil in your Divine Support System sessions, you may find it easily transports you into a meditative and receptive state, making your connection to the realm of spirits almost effortless over time.

Incense produces an aroma when burned and has been used in religious practices, rituals, and ceremonies for millennia. There are different types of incense, including stick incense, which is widely available and easy to burn in heat-proof incense holders. Burning powdered incense on heated charcoal may provide a purer expression of the scent since incense of this type doesn't contain fillers or additives. If you elect to use powdered incense, look to online videos for assistance and precautions.

Essential oils are derived from plants and are known to have healing properties. The aroma of essential oils can be disbursed using a diffuser. Alternatively, they can be applied directly onto the skin using a carrier oil, such as jojoba, to reduce the chance of skin irritation.

Here are but a few incense and essential oils for consideration:

Incense: Copal, frankincense, myrrh, pine

Essential Oils: Clary sage, frankincense, sandalwood, rosemary

Protection

Working with your Divine Support System doesn't require any extra energetic protection. However, you may wish to add an extra layer of energetic protection before engaging in specific communication methods described in chapter 7, such as the pendulum technique, automatic writing, or scrying. Establishing an energetic boundary ensures no unwanted or negative energies interfere with your healing session.

There are many options for creating a protective boundary against any negative or unwanted energies. If you currently perform rituals, such as the Lesser Banishing Ritual of the Pentagram, or if you are a Reiki healer familiar with using the Cho-Ku-Rei symbol for protection, you can employ whatever method is currently in your toolkit. In addition, here are three simple techniques that also effectively create energetic protection.

Smoke

This method uses your choice of incense or dried herbs, such as rosemary. Before lighting the incense or herb, state your intention that this smoke protects you and grants you safety from all negative energies and forces. Next, safely burn your incense or herb and allow the smoke to waft over you and the room that you are in. Take a moment to notice any shifts in energy within you and your space.

Circle of Golden Light

This technique requires your visualization skills. To begin, stand in front of the area where you'll communicate with your Divine Support System. After setting your intention to create a golden circle of protection, extend the arm of your dominant hand and walk clockwise in a large circle with your pointer finger extended. As you walk, visualize a beam of golden light streaming from your finger, creating a golden ring of light. As you do so, observe any shifts in your energy and the room's energy that may occur.

Divine Protection

This technique requires no specific metaphysical tools or skills. Although any protector deity can be called upon for assistance, Archangel Michael wielding his mighty sword is an excellent choice. Begin by setting your intention to call upon a specific spiritual protector to guard you and your space against negative energies. State aloud or silently your personal petition for safety, directed toward a specific deity, angel, or guide. Next, send your message of gratitude for the protection. When you have finished, pause a moment to observe any changes in your personal energy and the room's energy.

Your Personal Intention for Healing Sessions with Your Divine Support System

Our intention provides both focus and direction. Crafting an intention for each session with your Divine Support System assists with clearly defining your aims and objectives regarding your healing path. Composing your personal intention for a healing session is a separate practice from your heartfelt intention, which is your overarching objective for using this text.

Imagine your ultimate outcome: what do you want it to be? What steps to better health and wellness are you looking for assistance with right now? Be as specific as possible. Are you looking for general guidance regarding your overall health? Are you looking to start a new fitness routine and need extra motivation to do so? Your personal intention for a healing session can vary from day to day or remain relatively consistent and is based on your unique needs.

Sample Personal Intention for a Healing Session

It is my intention to meet with my Divine Support System today for assistance in reaching my health and wellness goals. First, I want to call upon Archangel Michael for the drive and motivation to start attending the gym consistently three times a week. Next, I desire to receive guidance from the centaur, Chiron, on the best options to help heal my digestive troubles and reduce the pain and inflammation in my belly. Finally, I will call upon Bast to help me reconnect to my sensual side, which has been neglected due to the pain and discomfort I have been experiencing. These are the steps I have determined will best assist me in reaching my long-term health and wellness goals.

Focusing Your Awareness

After you set your intention, the next step is to anchor yourself in the present moment. This action allows us to become more focused and aware of our physical, emotional, and psychic senses. Our thoughts are not projected into the future or dwelling in the past but centered in the here and now. Additionally, anchoring provides a stable foundation upon which we may commune with our Divine Support System.

You can perform your favorite grounding meditation or the suggested practice that follows, which also has the additional benefit of anchoring our awareness in both time and space. It combines a grounding breathing pattern, inhaling and exhaling through the nose for a count of four, projecting your awareness in all directions. It is a variation of the Seven Directions technique described by R. J. Stewart.[3] Here are the basic meanings:

Center: Denotes the core of your being, your essence, and your heart center

Before: Represents the cardinal direction (north, east, south, or west) in front of you and the future

Behind: Denotes the cardinal direction (north, east, south, or west) in the back of you and the past

---

3. R. J. Stewart, *Power Within the Land: Roots of Celtic and Underworld Traditions Awakening the Sleepers and Regenerating the Earth* (Rockport, MA: Element Books, 1992), 91.

Right: Represents the cardinal direction (north, east, south, or west) on your right side and your motivating force

Left: Denotes the cardinal direction (north, east, south, or west) on your left side and your receptivity

Above: Represents the direction above you and your connection to the Divine

Below: Denotes direct direction below you and your unrealized potential

EXERCISE
Centering Practice
to Align Yourself in Time and Space

1. Take a comfortable seat where you will not be disturbed, and ensure your cell phone is silenced.

2. Take a full breath in through your nose and exhale completely through your mouth.

3. Bring your awareness to your heart center. With your attention focused on your heart center, inhale through your nose for a count of four and exhale through your nose for a count of four.

4. Send your awareness from your heart center directly out in front of you while inhaling through your nose for a count of four. Exhale for a count of four through your nose, bringing your awareness back to your heart center.

5. Pause at your heart center, inhaling through your nose for a count of four and exhaling through your nose for a count of four.

6. Now, project your awareness from your heart center directly behind you, inhaling through your nose for a count of four.

Exhale through your nose for a count of four, inviting your awareness back to your heart center.

7. Pause at your heart center, inhaling through your nose for a count of four and exhaling through your nose for a count of four.

8. Send your awareness from your heart center toward the right while inhaling through your nose for a count of four. Exhale through your nose for a count of four, bringing your awareness back to your heart center.

9. Pause at your heart center, inhaling through your nose for a count of four and exhaling through your nose for a count of four.

10. Next, project your awareness from your heart center toward the left while inhaling through your nose for a count of four. Exhale through your nose for a count of four, inviting your awareness back to your heart center.

11. Pause at your heart center, inhaling through your nose for a count of four and exhaling through your nose for a count of four.

12. Send your awareness from your heart center directly above you while inhaling through your nose for a count of four. Exhale through your nose for a count of four, bringing your awareness back to your heart center.

13. Pause at your heart center, inhaling through your nose for a count of four and exhaling through your nose for a count of four.

14. Now, project your awareness from your heart center directly below you while inhaling through your nose for a count of four. Exhale through your nose for a count of four, inviting your awareness back to your heart center.

15. Finally, with your awareness focused on your heart center, inhale through your nose for a count of four and exhale through your nose for a count of four.

Opening Your Healing Session with Your Divine Support System

When you are ready to start your healing session with your Divine Support System, you should utilize an opening ritual signaling your intention to begin. If used consistently, this practice communicates to your Divine Support System your intention to start your session and prepares you for the encounter. Here are a few excellent ways to begin your healing session:

- Lighting a white candle
- Striking a Tibetan singing bowl with a mallet
- Using an opening gesture or symbol

If you are considering using an opening gesture or symbol, here are two suggestions, but feel free to experiment with other options.

Opening Gesture–Open Book: Hold your hands together with palms facing each other, fingers pointed away from you, and your thumbs facing up. Open your hands like a book and state, "Let's begin."

Opening Symbol–Infinity Compass: With your dominant hand's index and middle fingers, draw an infinity symbol in the air from top to bottom, from right to left, making an infinity cross. Small infinity loops will be drawn in the cross-quarters of the original infinity cross. This symbol helps you to connect to your life path and receive divine guidance associated with your personal evolutionary process. Once you have completed drawing your symbol of choice, you can state your intention to begin; for example, "Let us now begin our healing session."

At the close of your healing session, after expressing gratitude for the assistance of your Divine Support System, use the same method to signal the end of your session:

- Extinguish the white candle
- Strike a Tibetan singing bowl with a mallet
- Use a closing gesture or symbol

Closing Gesture–Closed Book: Hold your hands open like a book and slowly bring your palms together, your fingers pointed away from you, and your thumbs facing the ceiling. State, "We are finished."

Closing Symbol–Infinity Compass: Use the same method to draw the Infinity Compass. Then, state your intention to end the session by saying a phrase similar to "Let us end our healing session."

Are you ready to communicate with your Divine Support System? Let's begin.

Chapter 7

Techniques for Communicating with Your Divine Support System

There are many different methods of communicating with your Divine Support System. You may be drawn to one technique in particular based on your preferences and natural abilities. Focusing on one practice over time allows you to develop a deep understanding and level of comfort using the technique. Your proficiency and skill level will evolve over time.

Avoid alcohol or recreational drugs when communicating with your Divine Support System.

Petitions

A petition is a written request to a Divine Support System member for specific assistance or guidance. Petitions assist with clarifying your healing intention while working with that particular spirit helper and manifesting your healing goals. Always address a petition to a specific member of your Divine Support System and state your request in simple terms. When crafting a petition, writing from your heart and emotionally connecting to your request produces the best results.

You will need a piece of paper to connect with your Divine Support System through a petition. First, consider the type of paper you wish to use: colored, parchment, etc. To bring balance and connection to the earth element associated with manifestation, consider using a piece of paper that is square in shape, cutting to size if needed. Next, think about the color ink you will use. If your spirit ally is associated with a specific color, you may want to use ink that acknowledges this preference.

Consider lighting incense and a candle before you craft your petition to give your petition additional power. After you write your petition, you may anoint your petition with oil such as frankincense, myrrh, or olive oil. After completing it, you can roll up the piece of paper and tie it with ribbon or twine. Take a few moments of silence afterward to notice any shifts or changes you might experience due to writing your petition. Observe any intuitive messages or guidance you might receive through your psychic senses. Record your experiences in your healing journal. Finally, you can bury your petition in the earth or burn it safely in a controlled environment. Both methods help release the energy of the petition into the world where it can be manifested.

Sample petitions are found in chapter 11. As you will see, the samples are intended for guidance, not to be used word for word. Anything you write should be customized for your specific healing requests and goals.

Prayer

A prayer is a sincere request for assistance or an expression of gratitude to a higher power or deity. Alternatively, it can be thought of as a genuine desire or wish. Prayers have been used throughout human history and across cultures to communicate with the Divine.

You may have experience with formal prayers recited both publicly and privately in religious settings. If you are drawn to using these traditional prayers as a part of your communication with your Divine Support System, it is perfectly acceptable to do so. However, you may choose to design your own prayer based on your intentions for personal healing. Your sincerity is the key to crafting your personal prayers.

Prayers are not simply a list of demands given to the Divine to fulfill on your behalf. Your heart, not your ego, should be the driving force behind developing a personal prayer. Prayers should have an element of reverence and an acknowledgment that there is a power greater than

ourselves. You can refer to this higher power with any name that resonates with you, such as God, Source, Goddess, or Creator. Alternatively,
you can address your prayer to a specific member of your Divine Support
System. Expressing gratitude is another essential component to include
when designing your personal prayer. By being grateful for the blessings
we have already received, we open ourselves up to experience more benefits in the future.

If you design your own prayer for communicating with your Divine
Support System, write it down beforehand to ensure that it captures ex-
actly what you want to convey. Once you are satisfied with your personal
healing prayer, you can recite it each time you call upon your Divine
Support System. Here's a sample prayer for your consideration.

*Beloved Creator, I ask for your guidance and blessings as I walk
my path toward greater health and happiness. Please help me ac-
cept myself as I am now and fill me with your love. Please help me
make the necessary changes to attain my healing goals. I am grateful for my life, my healing journey, and all those human and divine
beings assisting me along my path.*

After reciting your prayer, take a few moments of silence afterward to
notice any shifts or changes you might experience. Observe any intuitive
messages or guidance you might receive through your psychic senses.
Lastly, record your experiences in your healing journal.

Dream Incubation

Dreams have a historical relationship to healing and communicating
with divine beings. As Robert Moss described in *The Secret History of
Dreaming*, ancient temples in Egypt (dedicated to Imhotep) and Greece
(dedicated to Asclepius) attracted pilgrims who traveled far and wide
to sleep within the temples to receive dreams of guidance and healing.
We can take a similar approach using the concept of dream incubation.
Dream incubation is the technique of obtaining advice or insights into
a specific question through dreams. Note that dream incubation is not

the same as lucid dreaming, the practice of becoming aware that you are dreaming within the dream and controlling the dream experience. To receive guidance, insights, and healing through dream incubation can be as involved or as simple as you choose.

Simple Dream Incubation Technique

This method requires no rituals or extra tools except your healing journal. Keep your healing journal and a writing utensil near your bed to easily record your experiences once you wake up. Begin by setting your intention to connect with a member of your Divine Support System to receive guidance, healing, or assistance with a specific element of your healing journey as you sleep. Alternatively, you can open the invitation to all members of your Divine Support System and ask that the spirit ally best suited to provide the assistance or guidance you need appear in your dream. Whisper your intention aloud before falling asleep, and repeat your request to yourself as you fall asleep. When you awake, document any dreams you might have experienced in your healing journal. If you don't remember your dream, write that in your healing journal and any feelings, emotions, or insights you have upon waking. The dream incubation technique is most effective when performed each night over a period of time.

Elaborate Dream Incubation Technique

This method establishes a routine to facilitate communication with your Divine Support System through dreams. Here are some ideas for establishing an environment that promotes effective dreaming and successful dream incubation.

> *Crystals:* Try placing one of these crystals under your bed or on your nightstand to increase your ability to connect with your dreams: amethyst, celestite, lapis lazuli, or tiger's eye.

Teas: Experiment with drinking a cup of tea before bed. Chamomile or lavender tea may help you achieve a more relaxed state. Mugwort tea is said to help with dream recall.

Herbs: Place a bowl of star anise on your nightstand to activate your intuition and facilitate prophetic dreams.

Essential Oils: Diffuse lavender, clary sage, jasmine, or sandalwood to promote the cultivation of a dream state.

Written Intention: Write your intention to connect with your Divine Support System in your dream on a piece of paper and sleep with it under your pillow.

To perform the elaborate dream incubation technique, any of the suggested elements can help with successful dream incubation before bedtime. After you lie down, whisper your intention to connect with a member of your Divine Support System to receive guidance, healing, or assistance with a specific element of your healing journey as you sleep. Alternatively, you can open the invitation to all members of your Divine Support System and ask that the spirit ally best suited to provide the needed assistance or guidance appear in your dream. Repeat your request to yourself as you fall asleep. When you awake, document any dreams you might have experienced in your healing journal. If you don't remember your dream, write that in your healing journal and any feelings, emotions, or insights you have upon waking.

Visualization

The visualization technique may be a fantastic place to start when first communicating with your Divine Support System. You don't need to purchase additional metaphysical tools. You only need your dynamic imagination and a quiet, safe space. The method is similar to daydreaming, except you will need a clear intention to maintain your focus.

Consider what setting you would like to use as your meeting place to invite members of your Divine Support System. Some suggestions are a chapel, a Greek temple, a pyramid, or a beach. A favorite location of mine is a garden full of flowers with a bench under a willow tree. Whatever setting you select, you should include a place for you and a member of your Divine Support System to sit.

Close your eyes and visualize your chosen location. Picture it as clearly as possible and hold your focus. Write down in your healing journal a description of your meeting place, and draw or sketch the setting if you are artistically inclined. Finally, make a few notes about how you felt while visualizing the scene and any physical reactions or random thoughts you may have experienced.

You are now ready to communicate with your Divine Support System using the visualization technique. If you'd like to allot a specific amount of time for your visualization, you can set a timer at the beginning of the session. You should have a particular guide, deity, angel, or another spiritual being in mind to invite into your meeting place. Before proceeding, ensure that you have already created your sacred space, set your personal healing intention, focused your awareness, and used an opening gesture or symbol.

1. Check your cell phone is silenced or turned off.
2. From a comfortable seated position, take a few deep, clearing breaths.
3. Gently close your eyes and picture your meeting place.
4. Now, envision yourself walking into your meeting place and taking a seat.
5. Spend a few moments noticing how you feel in the healing space you created.
6. When you are ready, invite in your selected member of your Divine Support System and ask the spiritual being to take the seat next to you.
7. Picture this spiritual being as clearly as you can.

8. Ask this spiritual being for healing, assistance, guidance, or protection based on your specific intention and healing goals.

9. Listen for a response. Be open to how you might receive this information. You may hear with your inner ears. You might see images that convey a message. You might have an inner knowing or feeling.

10. Once you feel that the healing session is at a close, thank the member of your Divine Support System and release the visualization.

11. After completing this practice, sit for a minute or two in reflection before journaling your experience in your healing journal.

Pendulum

The pendulum is a divination tool that can be used as a method to receive spiritual guidance. A pendulum is comprised of a small weight suspended from a chain or string, ideally three to six inches in length. If you are drawn to working with a pendulum for communication with your Divine Support System, it's best to have a dedicated pendulum used only for your healing sessions.

Selecting a pendulum is a personal choice. Pendulums are made from different metals and crystals. Use your intuition and choose the one that you are guided toward using. You can either purchase a pendulum or make one yourself. If you elect to make your own pendulum, you will need a piece of sturdy string or a chain and an object to attach to the end, such as a ring, washer, or key.

Once you have your pendulum, you will need to learn its language. Hold the pendulum by the string and ask that it show you "Yes." The pendulum may move in a circle or a horizontal line. Whatever the pendulum movement, that will be its response for "Yes." Next, establish the movement for "No." The movement the pendulum makes will be its specific "No" reply. You can proceed to ask several "Yes" or "No" questions to "test" your pendulum, such as "Is my name (insert your name)?" The pendulum may move slowly at first, which is entirely normal.

Once you have your baseline for "Yes" and "No," you can invite a Divine Support System member to provide you guidance. However, ensure that you have already created your sacred space, establish a layer of energetic protection, set your personal healing intention, focused your awareness, and used an opening gesture or symbol before proceeding.

There are many ways to use your pendulum to receive messages from your Divine Support System, including the following:

- Place the pendulum approximately five inches above the palm of your non-dominant hand and ask yes or no questions to a specific member of your Divine Support System about your healing path and health goals.
- Place the pendulum over food, drink, essential oils, crystals, etc., and ask yes or no questions to a specific member of your Divine Support System about whether these items would benefit you.

For more elaborate communication and specific guidance on using a pendulum, develop your own pendulum chart containing potential responses to your questions. Write down the possible answers to your inquiry on a piece of paper. Be as specific as possible. For example, ask your question aloud, then point to one response stating, "Is this the best path forward?" If the pendulum responds with "Yes," you have the answer. If the answer is "No," move to the subsequent potential response.

If you have issues with your pendulum not providing answers, it may need to be cleared of stagnant energies. You can clear the energy of your pendulum by placing it in fresh coffee grounds. Additionally, if your pendulum isn't moving, take a few moments to assess yourself. Are you feeling tired? Overwhelmed? Frustrated? If so, take a moment and try again later.

Automatic Writing

Also called psychography, automatic writing is another method that may be helpful when seeking guidance from your Divine Support System. In this practice, you clear your mind and allow yourself to compose written words without using your brain to write consciously. Instead, the words you write are inspired by a Divine Support System member. The primary benefit of this method is that you can receive detailed guidance and information. For many individuals, the chief obstacle is allowing the mind to quiet itself enough to allow the inspiration from your spiritual helper to flow through you and onto the paper. This technique requires a dedicated writing instrument and your healing journal. Alternatively, you can keep a separate notebook solely for automatic writing sessions.

When you are ready to communicate with your Divine Support System using the automatic writing technique, follow the steps below for your healing session. If you'd like to allot a specific amount of time for your automatic writing session, set a timer before you begin. You should have a particular guide, deity, angel, or other spiritual being in mind to give you the guidance you seek. Before proceeding, ensure that you have already created your sacred space, established a layer of energetic protection, set your personal healing intention, focused your awareness, and used an opening gesture or symbol.

1. Ensure your cell phone is silenced or turned off.
2. From a comfortable seated position, take a few deep, clearing breaths.
3. Pick up your dedicated writing utensil and healing journal or automatic writing notebook.
4. Spend a few moments allowing your mind to settle.
5. When your mind is clear and you feel ready, call upon the specific member of your Divine Support System and ask your question or ask for spiritual guidance.
6. You may decide to close your eyes or keep a soft gaze.
7. Allow your hand to write freely without actively thinking about what you are writing. It may take some time for the process of automatic writing to start. Be patient.
8. If your eyes are open, avoid looking at the page you are writing on.

9. Once you feel that the automatic writing session is at a close, thank the member of your Divine Support System.

10. Afterward, sit for a minute or two in reflection before reviewing the messages received through your automatic writing session.

The results of your automatic writing session may include phrases, symbols, and doodles. At first, the messages may not make sense; that's perfectly acceptable. However, the guidance you received may become more apparent over time. Reflect upon your results and document your experience in your healing journal.

If you have problems receiving results from your automatic writing session, try the process again. Automatic writing is a skill that takes practice. You may need to extend the time for quieting your mind. Taking a mindful walk before engaging in automatic writing is one way to clear your energy and focus your mind. Your ability to access guidance from your Divine Support System using automatic writing will develop over time.

Scrying

Scrying is receiving guidance, messages, or visions using the reflective surface of an object or an illuminated medium such as a candle. Scrying requires the scrying object, a light source, and a meditative state of mind. There are numerous types of scrying, a few of which are listed here.

Candle Gazing

Candle gazing is a form of scrying that involves gazing into a candle flame. You will need a candle and a lighter or matches to scry to use the candle gazing method. Here are the steps:

1. Silence your cell phone.

2. Set a timer for the length of time you are dedicating to your candle gazing practice.

3. Darken the room.

4. Sit comfortably.

5. Light your candle.

6. Soften your gaze.

7. Watch the candle flame dance.

8. If your mind wanders during this practice, refocus your attention on the candle flame.

9. At the close of your practice, record your experiences in your journal.

Using this technique over time, you may experience visions in the flame or gain other intuitive information through your psychic senses.

Water and Oil Gazing

Water and oil scrying consists of gazing into a bowl filled with water to which some olive oil or essential oil has been added. To scry using this method, you will need a bowl, water, your choice of oil, candles, and matches or a lighter. Here are the steps:

1. Silence your cell phone.

2. Set a timer for the length of time you are dedicating to your water and oil gazing practice.

3. Darken the room.

4. Sit comfortably.

5. Light your candle(s).

6. Pour the water into your bowl.

7. Place the candle or candles near your water bowl so that the light from the candles illuminates the water.

8. Add oil to the bowl filled with water.

9. Soften your gaze and gaze at the water within the bowl.

10. Observe the patterns and shapes of the oil within the water.

11. If your mind wanders during this practice, refocus your attention on the water.

12. At the close of your practice, record your experiences in your journal.

As you consistently practice using this method, you may experience visions or observe the appearance of images or symbols within the water. Alternatively, you may receive guidance through your psychic senses.

Crystal Gazing

Crystal gazing is a form of scrying that involves gazing into a crystal, usually in the shape of a sphere. You will need a crystal sphere, candles, matches, or a lighter to scry using the crystal gazing method. Consider the metaphysical properties of the crystal you would like to use for your scrying session. Three types of crystals that work exceptionally well for communicating with your Divine Support System. A listing of these crystals may be found below:

- *Smoky quartz*: Provides grounding, protection, and a sense of peace as you connect with your Divine Support System.
- *Black obsidian*: Offers protection, grounding, and added strength to your healing session.
- *Clear quartz*: Amplifies and assists with receiving clear messages from your Divine Support System.

To perform crystal gazing, follow these steps:

1. Silence your cell phone.
2. Set a timer for the length of time you are dedicating to your crystal gazing practice.
3. Darken the room.
4. Sit comfortably.
5. Light your candle(s).
6. Place the candle or candles near your crystal so that the light from the candles illuminates the crystal but is not reflected directly in the crystal itself.

7. Soften your gaze and observe the crystal.

8. If your mind wanders during this practice, refocus your attention on the crystal.

9. At the close of your practice, record your experiences in your journal.

Over time, you may experience visions in the form of smoke within the crystal, which may take the shape of specific images or symbols. Alternatively, you may receive guidance through your psychic senses as you perform crystal gazing.

Mirror Gazing

Mirror gazing is a form of scrying consisting of focusing on reflections in a mirror. To scry using the mirror method, you will need a round or oval portable mirror whose surface is regular or blackened (some individuals prefer obsidian, which I have found produces the best results), in addition to candles, matches, or a lighter. To perform mirror gazing, follow these steps:

1. Silence your cell phone.

2. Set a timer for the length of time you are dedicating to your mirror gazing practice.

3. Darken the room.

4. Sit comfortably.

5. Light your candle(s).

6. Place the candle or candles so that the light from the candles illuminates the mirror but is not reflected directly in the mirror itself.

7. Soften your gaze and observe the mirror.

8. If your mind wanders during this practice, refocus your attention on the mirror.

9. At the close of your practice, record your experiences in your journal.

Over time, you may experience visions of colors, images, geometric patterns, or symbols. Alternatively, you may receive guidance through your psychic senses.

Anatomy of a Scrying Session for Communicating with Your Divine Support System

When you are ready to communicate with your Divine Support System using a scrying technique, the following steps are always the same. Remember that if you'd like to allot a specific amount of time for your session, set a timer before you begin. You should have a particular guide, deity, angel, or another spiritual being in mind to ask for guidance and insights regarding your healing journey.

1. Ensure that you have created your sacred space.
2. Establish a layer of energetic protection.
3. Set your personal healing intention.
4. Focus your awareness.
5. Use an opening gesture or symbol.

When you are ready, scry with your Divine Support System:

1. Gather the materials you will need for your scrying session based on the type of scrying you will perform.
2. Check your cell phone is silenced or turned off.
3. Set up your materials and dim the lights.
4. From a comfortable seated position, take a few deep, clearing breaths.
5. Call upon the specific member of your Divine Support System and ask your question or ask for spiritual guidance.
6. Begin to gaze softly into your scrying device.
7. Allow yourself to observe any phenomena that may occur, such as mist or smoke, colors, geometric patterns, shapes, images, and symbols.

8. Allow yourself to receive intuitive messages and spiritual guidance through your psychic senses.

9. Once you feel that the scrying session is at a close, thank the member of your Divine Support System.

10. After completing this practice, sit for a minute or two in reflection before documenting your experiences in your healing journal.

If you experiment with one technique over a period of time but are not getting meaningful results, try a different method. Based on your natural aptitude, you may have faster results and receive more precise messages using a different technique. Keep experimenting until you find the approach that resonates with you.

Before continuing to the next chapter, experiment with a few different communication methods to see which ones are best suited for you. You can use one technique exclusively or explore combining various methods of communication. Once you select your preferred communication technique, we can establish meaningful relationships with your spirit allies and healing guides.

Chapter 8

Cultivate Relationships with Your Divine Support System

As you begin communicating with your Divine Support System members, consider the type of connection you wish to establish. Developing relationships with your Divine Support System is similar to establishing relationships with living people. New relationships begin as a meeting between strangers. From there, they may progress to casual acquaintances, moving toward established friendships that can be strengthened and grown into mentors, teachers, confidants, and best friends. The type of relationships you develop with your Divine Support System is a personal choice. However, if you desire to establish a strong bond with your spirit allies, there are some practices you might consider exploring.

Difference Between Worship and Reverence

Before diving deeper into ways to strengthen your relationships with members of your Divine Support System, we should review the difference between worship and reverence. Worship is the act of honoring God, Source, the Creator, the Goddess—whatever name you ascribe to the Highest Power. Depending on your chosen religion or spiritual practice, you may worship other deities within your selected pantheon. When working with our Divine Support System, we practice reverence instead of worship. With the exception of the deities of your chosen religion or spiritual practice, members of your Divine Support System should be offered deep respect and revered but not worshipped.

How do we express our reverence to members of our Divine Support System? Our deep admiration for our spirit allies is shown when we communicate with them in a respectful tone when using any of the communication techniques in chapter 7. It can also be attained by expressing appreciation for their assistance along your healing path and the blessings you have yet to receive. Moreover, our reverence can be demonstrated by our daily actions. Now, let's consider the various ways you can develop a close bond with your Divine Support System and show your deep respect for these powerful, healing spirit beings.

Research

One of the most effective ways to develop a close connection with your healing spirit allies is to learn about them. By showing interest in learning about the members of your Divine Support System, you express your willingness to deepen your relationship. Furthermore, the insights you gain from your knowledge may lead to more effective ways of working with these spirit allies and more success in achieving your healing goals. Below are suggestions for expanding your knowledge regarding specific types of members of your Divine Support System.

Personal Spirit Guides

The visualization technique in chapter 7 is the most effective way to know more about your personal spirit guides. With this method, you can meet and converse with your guide as you would a friend and establish a rapport. There are also several books on spirit guides and ways to communicate with them that may provide additional information as you develop and strengthen your bond with your personal spirit guides.

Ancestors

Since ancestors were once flesh and blood, there are various resources you can use to learn more about them. If you know your ancestors' names, you can research census data, obituaries, newspaper articles, ship manifests, and immigration records to learn more about their daily lives. There are websites dedicated to this type of research that can assist you. The more you discover about your ancestors, the easier it will be to establish a meaningful and beneficial relationship with them.

Deities

Fortunately, a wealth of material is available to those who wish to deepen their knowledge about a specific deity. From spiritual texts and epic poems to books focused on mythology, there is a host of reading material about deities by which you can enhance your knowledge and establish a strong foundation from which to develop your relationship.

Angels and Archangels

Many books have been written on angels and the angelic realms. There are even online courses to help you establish these connections. Research the angel(s) you chose as member(s) of your Divine Support System. Gustav Davidson's *A Dictionary of Angels* (Free Press, 1967) is a great place to start.

Ascended Masters

If you have elected to work with an Ascended Master as part of your Divine Support System, research if that Ascended Master ever lived as a human being. If so, you can research their incarnate life to gain insights. Many Ascended Masters use humans as channels to distribute their message—research to see if there are any books containing channeled messages from your selected Ascended Master.

Saints, Bodhisattvas, and Sages

These figures were all once human beings, and biographies may have been written about their lives. You can research different sources regarding their personal journey to cultivate a deeper awareness of them and an appreciation for their unique path that led them to be such powerful allies in healing.

Elementals

Knowledge about elementals can be obtained in various ways. Spending time interacting with the associated element of the elemental is a way of having a personal experience of the elemental's essences and establishing a rapport. Alternatively, you can find books about the elementals from sources such as *Paracelsus, the Four Elements and Their Spirits* by Manly P. Hall and *Enchantment of the Faerie Realm* by Ted Andrews. A fun way to approach the world of the elementals and form a deeper bond with these helpful spirit allies is by reading fairy tales and myths connected to the element or associated elemental.

Crystal and Plant Allies

Plants and crystals have associated healing and metaphysical properties. You can learn about these attributes using an online search. For a deeper understanding, consider expanding your research to books specializing in the healing properties of crystals or plants. *The Book of Stones: Who They Are and What They Teach Us* by Robert Simmons and Naisha Ahsian is an excellent resource on crystals. If you are interested in learning more about the healing and metaphysical properties of plants, there are wonderful books regarding the use of herbs and flowers, essential oils, and flower essences. Additionally, you can develop a relationship and learn more about the healing benefits of plants and crystals by meditating while holding a crystal or plant in your hand and opening yourself up to receive intuitive guidance and messages.

Animal Spirit Helper

If an animal spirit helper is a member of your Divine Support System, learn details about the animal, such as its appearance, characteristics, and habitat. Watching documentaries may be a valuable way of gaining insights into the nature of a specific animal. Myths and fables featuring your animal are another way to establish an understanding of the animal's nature. Books that detail the attributes associated with animal spirit helpers may provide additional information that will assist you in establishing a relationship.

Altars

When establishing your relationship with your Divine Support System, you may decide to create an altar, a dedicated place to connect with your spirit healing allies. Various religions and other spiritual practices use altars as structures or platforms for worship or manifesting. An altar can be permanent or temporary. It can be simple or elaborate. An altar can be a shelf on your bookshelf, a scarf laid on your bureau, or a coffee table. There are no set rules to follow when creating an altar to connect with your Divine Support System. Listen to your intuition and create one that feels appropriate for you. Some of the items most commonly included on altars are candles, incense, pictures or paintings, statues or figurines, flowers, and crystals or stones.

Although there is no set of rules regarding the creation of an altar, there is a practice you should follow if you decide to incorporate an altar into your Divine Support System practice. Keep your altar clean and free of dust. By maintaining your healing altar, you show your Divine Support System that you also care for your relationships with them.

Offerings

As gifts to members of your Divine Support System, offerings are a physical representation of your desire to show your appreciation, commitment to your healing journey, and connection to your Divine Support System members. You can give offerings ranging from flowers to food, jewelry to coins. The only rule is that once an offering is made, it cannot be reused for another purpose.

When selecting the offering to present to your Divine Support System, think of offerings that are based on the type of spirit ally they are meant for. If you are working with a spirit helper listed in chapters 10 through 12, suggested offerings are provided for your consideration. When presenting an offering to ancestors, consider an offering of coins or a handmade gift. Trust your intuition during the offering selection process—your inner guidance may draw you toward an offering that may be unconventional yet appropriate for you. When in doubt, a simple offering of clear water is a suitable choice.

Food and drink are common and effective offerings to present to your Divine Support System. Your spirit helpers do not physically consume these offerings but instead receive sustenance by absorbing the items' energy. When they are finished, disposing of food and drink offerings doesn't have to be complicated: State that you are disposing of these items and that you hope your spirit allies enjoyed them and have taken their fill. You can then dispose of the items in the trash or compost them if appropriate. There is some dispute regarding disposing of food and drink offerings in this manner; however, I have found it both practical and helpful in preventing littering.

Activities for Alignment

Another way to strengthen your bond with a specific member of your Divine Support System is to engage in activities connected to their interests and passions. This practice assists with aligning your physical, emotional, mental, and spiritual energies with your selected member of your Divine Support System. When you perform the activity, you signal your willingness to connect to a specific member of your Divine Support System and show your commitment to your healing journey.

Selecting an activity shows your knowledge about your spirit ally and demonstrates your dedication to developing a relationship. For example, suppose you are creating a relationship with an animal spirit helper. In that case, you may adopt a vegan/vegetarian lifestyle or say a prayer of gratitude honoring the animal's life before consuming meat. In addition, many of the spirit ally descrptions in chapter 10 include suggested activities for aligning with the energies of these divine spirit helpers.

Putting It All Together:
Sample Healing Session with Your Divine Support System

Here is a suggested outline for your healing session with your Divine Support System. The invitation is to develop your own practice using the methods that resonate with you. Your healing session can be as quick as ten minutes or as long as an hour, based on what elements you add to it.

1. Silence or turn off your cell phone.

2. Set up your altar.

3. Light incense or diffuse an essential oil.

4. Create sacred space using the White Light method described in chapter 2 or your chosen method.

5. If using a pendulum, automatic writing, or scrying, use a form of energetic protection.

6. Set up your personal intention for this healing session.

7. Focus your awareness using the Centering practice described in chapter 2.

8. Perform the opening gesture or opening symbol signaling the start of your healing session.

9. Present any offerings you may be giving to your Divine Support System members and set them on your altar or in front of you.

10. Communicate with your Divine Support System using your selected method: petition, prayer, visualization, pendulum, automatic writing, or scrying. Multiple methods can be used in one session, time permitting.

11. Spend a few moments reflecting upon your experience before documenting your session in your healing journal.

12. Express gratitude for the assistance of your Divine Support System and your journey toward greater health and well-being.

13. Perform the closing gesture or closing symbol.

Remember that your relationship with your Divine Support System members is based on your dedication, effort, and desire. The more time and attention you devote to activities associated with your Divine Support System, the more successful the outcome.

Chapter 9
Seven Keys to Success

There are seven keys that will ensure the best results for working with your Divine Support System. These elements can prompt a more productive and effective healing journey. They aren't shortcuts to instant results but are practices and mindsets that provide the framework for achieving a rewarding and healing experience with your Divine Support System.

Key One: Your Healing Journal

Your healing journal is the number one tool for your sessions with your Divine Support System. It tracks your goals, intentions, the members of your Divine Support System, and your outcomes. Over time, it will be a tremendous resource for you, so continue to document your journey.

Your healing journal can include a daily diary of your healing path that includes dreams, insights, any activities you will be engaged in to connect with your Divine Support System, and a log of how you feel physically, mentally, emotionally, and spiritually. It should also include notes on all your healing sessions with your Divine Support System. Here are some recommended items to include in your journal when documenting a healing session.

Date and Time

Including the date and time in your healing journal helps you to track your progress. You may want to include the sun's placement in the sky by writing down which zodiac sign the sun is in. You might also want to record the phase of the moon.

Daily Healing Intention

This intention might be consistent from day to day, or you may tweak it based on your current needs. By recording it in your healing journal, you can assess what intentions were more powerful and produced the best results over time.

Members of Your Divine Support System

List the current members of your Divine Support System and how you will work with them for greater health and happiness. It's important to know what assistance each healing ally is being asked to perform so that you can track the effectiveness of your collaboration with that healing ally.

Your Current Condition

Document your physical, mental, emotional, and spiritual condition before and after any healing sessions with your Divine Support System. Both subtle and significant shifts can occur during your healing sessions, and recording your before and after states of being is an invaluable tool for evaluating these changes.

Communication Methods

Record your chosen way of communicating with your Divine Support System, including your results and how you felt during the communication portion of your healing session.

Experiences, Insights, and Guidance

Document your experiences during your healing session, including any insights or guidance from your psychic senses. Even if the information you received doesn't make sense now, you may find that the messages from your Divine Support System may become clear as you proceed further down your path toward greater health and well-being.

Overall Impression of Experience

In addition to your experiences and any information you received, it's also a good idea to record your overall impression of your healing session. Consistent feedback will help you identify what works best for you and any areas you want to adjust in the future.

Remember that your healing journal is personal to you. If you'd like to include items not listed here, such as sketches, meaningful poems, or pressed flowers or herbs, by all means, do so. Your healing journal will become the story of your growth and personal evolution. Review it often and marvel at your progress along your healing path.

Key Two: Demands versus Requests

Your tone matters. Consider the type of voice you use when asking a friend or family member for help. What would the response be if you made demands in a loud voice? The same is true when communicating with your Divine Support System. When you need help from your Divine Support System, you are not demanding that they help you—instead, you are requesting assistance.

Communication is a significant component of any relationship between colleagues, family members, or friends. Your relationships with members of your Divine Support System are no exception. A sincerely worded prayer or heartfelt petition reflecting a tone of reverence will receive a more attentive and supportive response than a forcefully expressed command.

As you communicate with your Divine Support System from your heart, open yourself up to listen to their messages as you request their assistance. Communication is a two-way street alternating between speaking and listening. After communicating with a member of your Divine Support System, whether through petition, prayer, or another means, open yourself up to listen for a response. Pay attention to your physical body, emotions, and thought patterns for an intuitive answer to your request. Don't limit yourself by only looking for an immediate response after requesting assistance from your Divine Support System; you might also receive a reply in your dreams. By asking and not demanding, we open ourselves up to experience the realization of our healing goals and the deepening of our relationships with our Divine Support System.

Key Three: Consistency

If you want tangible results and lasting change, developing a consistent schedule for your healing sessions with your Divine Support System is critical. Whether you decide to do small daily practices or a more extended weekly session, your schedule should fit your lifestyle. Consider the following topics when establishing a consistent routine to meet with your Divine Support System.

Be Realistic

When we start a new and exciting course of action, we can develop lofty goals and be overly optimistic about what can be accomplished in a day. Pause and consider how much time each day or each week you can realistically dedicate to communing with your Divine Support System. Could you devote fifteen minutes each night before bed and a half hour on the weekends? Can you commit to three twenty-minute sessions a week? The choice is yours, but starting with smaller, realistic goals may be best for developing the consistency needed to establish meaningful, productive relationships with your Divine Support System members.

Create a Schedule

After determining the amount of time available to dedicate to communing with your Divine Support System, the next step is to schedule your sessions. Consider your natural rhythm: Are you a morning person? If so, perhaps getting up fifteen minutes earlier than usual will allow you to seamlessly fit in your healing sessions first thing in the morning before the hustle and bustle of the day divert you. If you tend to feel more energized at night, your healing sessions could easily become part of your nighttime routine. Maybe you can schedule a meeting with yourself during your lunch hour and dedicate a half hour of that time to communing with your Divine Support System. Plan your sessions in a planner or an online calendar to track your upcoming healing sessions and set reminders to help keep you on track. Permit yourself to modify your schedule as needed, but hold yourself accountable.

Develop a Plan for the Unexpected

Our lives are constantly in flux and change. As a result, unexpected situations may pop up, preventing us from sticking to our regular routines. Scheduled healing sessions might be missed due to any number of reasons, but we can develop a plan to address this issue. Craft a short declaration to your Divine Support System that you can use as a substitute for your healing session, such as "Although I was not able to join my Divine Support System today for our healing session, I am committed to my healing path, dedicated to developing relationships with my Divine Support System, and delighted to restart our journey tomorrow." A simple acknowledgment of your commitment will maintain your momentum and keep moving you toward your healing goals.

Once you build momentum and experience positive results, communing with your Divine Support System will become a healthy habit and part of your lifestyle.

Key Four: Gratitude Mindset

Previously, it was suggested that a statement of thanks for the assistance of your Divine Support System should always conclude your healing sessions Saying *thank you* assures your spirit helpers that their help is valued and may motivate them to provide additional blessings. However, there are significant benefits to cultivating gratitude throughout the day, not just for a brief moment during your healing sessions. In *The Psychology of Gratitude* (UK: Oxford University Press, 2004), Robert Emmons and Michael McCullough present the numerous health and social benefits resulting from a gratitude mindset. Some advantages of a sincere gratitude practice include the following:

- Increases your ability to enjoy life
- Decreases the impact of stress on daily life
- Promotes optimism about the future
- Elevates energy levels
- Improves sleep quality and duration
- Enhances the quality of relationships
- Encourages compassion and empathy
- Promotes healthier lifestyle options
- Increases self-confidence

Since there are so many benefits to cultivating a mindset of gratitude, it's a good idea to express thanks to your Divine Support System at various times throughout the day, and there are many ways to do so. Consider writing a message of gratitude to your Divine Support System in your healing journal each day. You may wish to develop an affirmation you can repeat throughout the day, such as "I am full of gratitude for my healing journey and for the limitless blessings I receive from my Divine Support System." Additionally, you might compose a thank-you letter to a specific member of your Divine Support System if you receive exceptional guidance or assistance with reaching a healing goal. By using simple practices to bring more gratitude into your life, you will be better able to receive healing gifts from your spirit allies.

Key Five: Suspension of Disbelief and Cultivating Faith

Faith and belief are essential to manifest our inner vision into the material world. Faith and belief in the unseen realms can sometimes be challenging. How do we know our spirit allies are assisting us if we can't see them with our physical eyes or hear them with our physical ears? To bridge between doubt and faith, we must suspend our disbelief.

Set the intention to permit yourself to believe in the unseen realms and your spirit allies until you have established confidence in their existence. If you enjoy visualizations, you can imagine a box where you can place your doubts and skepticism, knowing you can retrieve them any-time. Use your creativity to develop a method that works best for you.

Remember that developing faith takes time. Be patient with yourself and trust that your direct experience with communing with your Divine Support System will have tangible benefits that will convert you into a believer (if you have yet to become one).

Key Six: Desire

Desire may be defined as a powerful feeling of wishing, wanting, or crav-ing something. Your desire to communicate with and receive blessings from your Divine Support System can affect the effectiveness of your healing sessions and provide inspiration and energy, propelling you along your healing path toward greater health and happiness. Desire is intimately connected with emotions and thoughts. By tapping into your desire and cultivating its unique power, the energy created can serve as the necessary fuel to manifest our biggest dreams.

Before and during your sessions with your Divine Support System, tap into your genuine desire for healing and your deepest wish for con-nection with your spirit allies. This extra energy boost associated with your intense desire can be the stimulus for more dynamic healing ses-sions. When your heartfelt desire is combined with consistent healing sessions with your Divine Support System, you will have more successful and tangible results.

Key Seven: Curiosity

Developing an inquisitive mind opens up new possibilities and areas of exploration for personal growth and healing opportunities. By approach-ing your Divine Support System with curiosity, you are increasing your level of engagement with your spirit allies. A curious attitude promotes collaboration, teamwork, and connection with your spirit helpers.

When we engage with our curious nature, we open ourselves up to possibilities, making it one of the best catalysts for success in reaching goals of greater health and well-being. You can include curiosity as part of your healing journey with your Divine Support System in several ways, including the following:

- Thinking about the unseen realms and how they might interact with your reality
- Curiosity about the members of your Divine Support System and how they can assist you in reaching your healing goals
- Inquiring how you might receive messages and guidance from your spirit allies
- Exploring how you might experience greater health and happiness

Follow your healing path with dedication, gratitude, faith, desire, and curiosity; you will successfully transform your life into one filled with greater health and happiness with the unlimited support of your Divine Support System.

Chapter 10

Healing Deities, Ascended Masters, Angels, and More

Although no single text can provide a complete listing of all divine beings that can assist you along your path to greater health and well-being, this listing may provide inspiration regarding potential members of your Divine Support System. If a healing ally appeals to you, do further investigation and research the mythos surrounding that spirit, strengthening your connection. Enjoy the journey!

Aceso (Deity, Greek)

Aceso is a Greek goddess of healing, and one of five daughters of the legendary Greek physician, Asclepius. Each of Asclepius's daughters represented a different aspect of medicine and healing. The caring goddess, Aceso, is the personification of the healing process, from the illness's inception through the treatment phase to the return to optimal health. Aceso can be called upon to assist with the healing process and recovery after an illness or injury.

To connect with the healing energies of the goddess Aceso, try the following:

- Engage in self-care practices, such as taking a restorative bath, receiving a massage, or taking a gentle walk in nature

- Place carnations (a flower considered sacred in ancient Greece) in a prominent place in your home
- Meditate upon your body's incredible capacity to heal

Here's a sample personal petition to Aceso:

Goddess Aceso, daughter of Asclepius, please hear my request. My physical body requires profound healing, and I ask that you actively participate in my healing journey. Please guide me to better health and share your healing wisdom with me so that I can be a more en-gaged participant in my own healing process. Please send me healing energies to aid my return to optimal health and enhance my overall well-being. Thank you. Thank you. Thank you.

Áine (Deity, Irish)

An Irish goddess of love and fertility, Áine (pronounced "ON-ya") is also referenced as a fairy queen who is associated with the summer season, abundance, and personal sovereignty. In ancient Gaelic, her name means "bright" or "delight." Some believe that Áine is a reinterpretation of a more ancient mother goddess, Danu.

Áine is an independent goddess who is reported to have romantic ad-ventures with both deities and humans, producing human offspring. She is celebrated on Midsummer's Eve with processions of torches to invoke fertility and productivity. Her mythology includes her connection to the legendary King of Munster, who is reported to have assaulted Áine, prompting her to bite off his ear. Due to an Irish law stating that only a person without a blemish can rule, the king was removed from power.

Áine can be called up to help heal a broken heart, for protection, for fertility issues, to experience more joy in life, to recover after sexual abuse or trauma, to enhance creativity, to heal animals and the environ-ment, and to attract abundance.

To bond with the loving energies of Áine, consider trying the following:

- Listen to traditional Irish folk music
- Spend time in a park or garden appreciating the flowers

- Plant and nurture a fuchsia plant, a sacred plant of Ireland
- Meditate with crystals, such as red marble and amber

If you'd like to craft a personal petition to Áine, here's one example:

Goddess Áine, Fairy Queen of Munster, please hear my words. Turn your loving gaze upon me and assist me with achieving my heart's desire for healing my wounded heart. Please help me completely recover from past trauma, find joy in life, and move forward with confidence, clarity, and alignment with my divine purpose. I also ask for your protection today and all my days. Thank you. Thank you. Thank you.

Airmid (Deity, Irish)

Airmid is a powerful Celtic goddess who may transmit secret teachings of healing. She is a member of the group of Celtic beings called the Tuatha Dé Danaan and is the daughter of the divine master physician, Dian Cécht. She is well-known for her healing abilities, especially using the power of plants and herbs for healing purposes. Unfortunately, the story of her myth illustrates extreme family dysfunction: Dian Cécht became jealous of the healing abilities of his daughter and son, Airmid and Miach, and eventually killed Miach. Watered by Airmid's tears, healing plants sprouted on the top of Miach's burial mound. Airmid then collected these plants, understanding their healing properties. However, still enraged at his children, Airmid's father scattered the herbs, and their healing remedies were lost.

Airmid can be a dynamic spiritual helper and is willing to share the lost knowledge of the healing benefits of plants and flowers with those who connect to her energies. She can assist with overall healing, healing family relationships, grief, depression, and recovering from family trauma.

You can connect with the healing energies of the goddess Airmid in many ways, including the following:

- Learn about healing herbs, flowers, and plants
- Use the healing benefits of plants (e.g., essential oils, teas, flower essences, and more)
- Create a simple altar to Airmid decorated with dandelions (a master healer of the plant world) or another healing herb or flower as the focal point
- Meditate with stones such as peach calcite and moss agate

Craft a personal petition to Airmid such as the following:

Goddess Airmid of the Tuatha Dé Danaan, please hear my humble request. I have embarked on a path of healing, both for myself and to help others. I feel a connection with you and hope that we can form a meaningful relationship. Please share your secret healing teachings with me so that I can actively participate in my own healing and assist others. Thank you. Thank you. Thank you.

Apollo (Deity, Greek)

Worshiped as a sun god and associated with music, prophecy, medicine, and healing, Apollo is linked to the sun's healing properties, including its restorative and regenerative benefits. He is considered the most beautiful of the gods, often depicted without a beard and wearing a crown of laurel leaves, holding a lyre or a bow. He can be pictured riding in a chariot pulled by celestial steeds.

Although willing to provide protection and healing to those who ask for assistance, Apollo is known to be vengeful, inflicting plagues and diseases on his enemies. Additionally, he contributed to the world of healing as the father of Asclepius, the god of healing and medicine. Apollo can assist with overall healing, issues with fatigue, personal power, vitality, depression, and problems pertaining to self-confidence.

If you'd like to explore the energies of Apollo, consider the following suggestions:

- Spend time in the sun (safely, using the appropriate protection such as sunblock and hats)
- Connect with the image of the sun by meditating on its classical glyph of a circle with a dot in the middle of it
- Connect with crystals associated with Apollo and the healing qualities of the sun, such as amber, citrine, and sunstone
- Read the Orphic Hymn to Apollo, number 33
- Meditate on the color gold or incorporate more gold-colored clothing into your wardrobe

If you'd like to craft a personal petition to Apollo, here's one example:

Apollo, Golden One, Lord of the Sun, please turn your gaze toward me. I come seeking your favor and blessings. Shine your brilliant light upon me, increasing my health and vitality. Help me step into the sun and stand in my personal power with confidence. Please strengthen my healing abilities and awaken new knowledge of healing practices so I may continue further down my healing path and be of service to others. Thank you. Thank you. Thank you.

Artemis (Deity, Greek)

Artemis is a virgin moon goddess of Greek origins. She can be visualized as a young, confident female hunter roaming the forests with her bow and arrows. Artemis is known as the protector of pregnant and newborn animals. She also has a deep connection with pregnancy and fertility, which is illustrated in her myth by describing how she acted as a midwife to the birth of her twin, Apollo .

A common theme in the myths associated with Artemis is her protecting her virtue from would-be aggressors. In one legend, the mythic hunter Orion assaulted Artemis, who, rather than succumbing to his advances, took his life. In another myth, Orion boasted that he could hunt every animal on earth, which earned him the wrath of Gaia (protector goddess of the earth and all the creatures inhabiting it), Leto (Artemis's mother, a nymph), and Artemis herself. As revenge, Gaia sent a giant scorpion to kill Orion. When it succeeded, the goddesses placed Orion's body in the heavens along with the scorpion that took his life. Artemis is an example of a deity embracing both strength and compassion.

Artemis can assist with the healing of sexual abuse, the overall health of young girls and young women, fertility issues, connecting to your personal power, boundary issues, assistance with pregnancy and childbirth, and healing animals.

If you'd like to connect with the powerful and protective energies of Artemis, try the following activities:

- Place a small statue or image of a stag or hawk, traditional symbols associated with Artemis, on a small altar dedicated to the goddess
- Give an offering of honey or fresh honeycomb to Artemis
- Read the Orphic Hymn to Artemis, number 36
- Donate to a local animal shelter that cares for dogs, an animal sacred to Artemis

You could also create a personal petition to Artemis; here is one example:

Hear my words, beautiful goddess Artemis of the forest. As you roam and hunt under the moon's light, cast your loving gaze in my direction. It is my intention to develop a relationship with you and work with your powerful healing energies. Please banish past traumas and current illnesses from all layers of my being. Please assist in restoring me to radiant health so I can live a life of harmony and balance. Thank you. Thank you. Thank you.

Asclepius (Deity, Greek)

Asclepius is a Greek god often called the Father of Medicine. One version of his legend says he was a gifted child educated in the healing arts by the centaur, Chiron. Asclepius became such a skilled healer that he could raise the dead, which angered Hades, the god of the dead. Hades brought this transgression to Zeus, who decided that Asclepius had become too powerful and thus struck him with a bolt of lightning, ending his life. However, Asclepius was rewarded for his contributions to humanity by being elevated to the rank of god so he could act as a divine healer and physician. Asclepius is often depicted with a snake or a dog holding a healing staff.

Asclepius used dreams and herbal remedies to cure those who petitioned him for assistance. Asclepius's cults were numerous and spread from Greece to Egypt to England. Those seeking healing would often travel to a temple dedicated to Asclepius, where they would sleep in the temple overnight and have their dreams interpreted by a priest of Asclepius, hoping to receive a cure for their affliction.

Asclepius can be petitioned for all types of healing: physical, mental, emotional, and spiritual. He can also assist with the healing of others and help healers strengthen their healing abilities and knowledge of different healing modalities.

To explore the healing energies of Asclepius, consider the following suggestions:

- Connect with your dreams by keeping a dream journal
- Study herbal remedies and botany
- Read the Orphic Hymn to Asclepius, number 67
- Diffuse essential oils such as cypress and sage

If you'd like to write a personal petition to Asclepius, here's one example:

Asclepius, Father of Medicine, please hear my words. Student of Chiron, grant me the knowledge of healing. Please help me learn the remedies that will be most beneficial to me. Please help me to receive messages of healing in my dreams. Grant me the blessing of health and well-being that allows me to be of service to humanity. I am grateful for your blessings and presence in my life. Thank you. Thank you. Thank you.

Babaji (Ascended Master)

Babaji or Mahavatar Babaji is an Ascended Master first reported in the best-selling book *Autobiography of a Yogi* by Paramahansa Yogananda. *Maha* means "great," and *avatar* describes the descent of a deity to Earth or the manifestation of a deity in human form, while *Babaji* translates to "Father" or "Grandfather." As a result, Babaji can be described as the Great Incarnate Father.[4]

According to Babaji's mythology, he was born with the name Nagaraj in 203 CE in Tamil Nadu, India. Upon reaching the age of fifteen, he left home in pursuit of spiritual knowledge. Babaji studied yoga, including breathwork, meditation, and body postures to unite the mind, body, and spirit. Over time, he became a master yogi and settled in the Himalayas, where he dove even deeper into his spiritual practices, becoming a *Siddha*, a being of enlightenment.

Babaji can assist with overall healing, strengthening the mind-body-spirit connection, depression, anxiety, healing of relationships, forgiveness, and connection to divine love.

To connect with the loving and supportive energies of Babaji, consider the following activities:

- Light a white candle in Babaji's honor
- Practice a mind-body-spirit form of physical exercises, such as yoga, tai chi, and qigong
- Spend time in silent meditation
- Read *Autobiography of a Yogi* by Paramahansa Yogananda
- Practice random acts of kindness

Here's one example of a personal petition to Babaji:

Dearest Babaji, please hear this request made with an open heart. Please come to me as a healer and a teacher. Please strengthen my mind-body-spirit connection and deepen my connection to the Di-

---

4. Kyle Gray, *Divine Masters, Ancient Wisdom: Activations to Connect with Universal Spiritual Guides* (Carlsbad, CA: Hay House, 2021), 105.

*vine. Please bring balance and harmony to my life and my rela-
tionships. Please lead me down the path to greater wellness and
happiness, assisting me with reaching my healing goals. With a
grateful heart, I give you thanks. Thank you. Thank you. Thank you.*

Barbara (Saint)

Saint Barbara was reportedly kept in a tower by her pagan father to keep
her safe from being kidnapped by prospective suitors. However, even
suitors who did meet her father's approval were continually rejected, as
Barbara had made a secret pledge to Jesus to remain pure. When her
father was away, Barbara left the tower and was privately baptized by a
priest (in some accounts, herself). She proceeded to destroy all of her father's pagan idols.

When her father returned, he was so enraged that he attempted to kill
Barbara, but she was miraculously saved and escaped. However, a shep-
herd revealed her hiding place, and she was taken to jail, where miracles occurred. First, the staves wielded to strike Barbara were changed
into peacock feathers. Next, when her torturers went to burn her, their
torches were mysteriously extinguished. Additionally, any wounds Barbara received were instantaneously healed. The judge offered Barbara's
father the option of executing her in private, which he accepted. Upon a
mountain, Barbara's father proceeded to take her life. As he did, he was
immediately struck by lightning and died.

Saint Barbara can assist with miraculous physical healing, protection
of your physical body from harm, fertility issues, alleviation of suffering,
healing of relationships, standing in your personal power, strength, confidence, and the healing of children.

Here's a partial list to align with the healing and protective energies of
Saint Barbara:

- Light a red candle in her honor
- Give offerings to Saint Barbara, such as a miniature tower,
  honeysuckle flowers, and peacock feathers

- Meditate on an image or statue of Saint Barbara
- Play golf—Saint Barbara is the matron saint of golfers

Here's an example of a personal petition to Saint Barbara:

Dearest Saint Barbara, I seek your strength, power, and blessings. As you received extraordinary healing, please assist me in obtaining miraculous healing on all levels of my being: physical, emotional, mental, and spiritual. Please grant me the courage to face all adversities and the strength to succeed in all my endeavors. Finally, please provide me with your protection today and all my days. I am very grateful for your presence in my life and assistance with my healing journey. Thank you. Thank you. Thank you.

Bastet (Deity, Egyptian)

Bastet was initially depicted as a solar lion goddess but eventually transformed into a feline deity associated with the moon. As the daughter of the sun god, Ra, she was gifted with the Eye of Horus, the all-seeing eye representing health, protection, and healing. Bastet presides over pleasure, sensuality, and joy. With her affiliation to the moon, she may also assist with intuition and magic.

Although no longer envisioned as a lion goddess, Bastet is still a goddess of protection, especially for women and children. During the period of the Pyramid texts, approximately 2613–2181 BCE, Bastet was described as the young king's nursemaid and protector in adulthood. In the Egyptian Coffin texts (written approximately 2100 BCE), she is also associated with the role of guardian and protector of the dead.

Bastet can be called upon to assist with all types of healing, protection, fertility issues, depression, sexual issues, healing from sexual trauma, strengthening intuition, and generating more joy and pleasure in life.

To connect with the healing and protective energies of Bastet, try the following:

- Donate to a local animal shelter dedicated to the welfare of cats
- Explore your sensual side through movement, physical touch, eating decadent food, and wearing luxurious clothing
- Develop your intuition by listening to your gut response
- Meditate with crystals like tiger's eye, carnelian, or jasper

You could also design a personal petition to Bastet; here's one example:

Bastet, Mistress of Oracles, please hear my petition. I wish to form a relationship with you for the purpose of healing and personal growth. Please assist me along my healing path by strengthening my physical body, emotional intelligence, and intuition. Please help me to invite more joy into my daily life and reclaim my sensual nature. Finally, please protect my body, mind, and soul today and all my days. Thank you. Thank you. Thank you.

Black Madonna (Deity)

The Black Madonna is a controversial figure related to the representation of Madonna, the mother of Jesus Christ, with a non-traditional portrayal. Approximately 250 Black Madonna statues, icons, and paintings exist primarily in Europe and Latin America. The term *black* doesn't necessarily refer to the color; however, there are images of the Black Madonna that do represent women from the sub-Saharan region. Black Madonnas may be depicted with black, brown, gray, or another skin tone. Additionally, the term *black* also denotes something hidden or mysterious. There are legends of Black Madonnas spontaneously appearing in caves, trees, and hidden places.

The identity of the woman depicted as the Black Madonna is also disputed. Theories range from Mary, mother of Jesus, to Mary Magdalene, to Pagan deities the Church deemed forbidden. Despite this controversy, the miracles associated with the Black Madonna are well known, and visitations to her shrines are popular tourist attractions. A few notable

Black Madonnas are the Black Madonna of Czestochowa in Poland, the Black Madonna of Guadalupe in Cáceres, Spain, and the Black Madonna of Orcival in France.

Black Madonna can help with healing and protect all levels of being: physical, mental, emotional, and spiritual. She can alleviate depression and anxiety. She can heal body-image issues, mother-child relationships, fertility problems, and recovery after sexual trauma. Black Madonna is a powerful ally for breaking the bonds of addiction and compulsive behaviors, and she can help you stand in your personal power and connect to the divine feminine.

To explore the powerful and healing energies of the Black Madonna, consider the following activities:

- Meditate using a picture or statue of a Black Madonna
- Place roses in a prominent area of your home
- Donate to charities that assist women and children
- Meditate with crystals associated with the energies of Black Madonna, such as black tourmaline, black moonstone, and rose quartz

Here is an example of a personal petition to the Black Madonna:

Dearest Black Madonna, Compassionate One, please grant me your blessings, power, and favor. Please provide me with miraculous healing on all levels of my being: physical, mental, emotional, and spiritual. Please strengthen my connection to the Divine and the divine feminine within me. Please fill me with divine grace and love so I can be a beacon of love and light to others. I am grateful for your presence in my life and your assistance in helping me reach my healing goals. Thank you. Thank you. Thank you.

Bona Dea (Deity, Roman)

Bona Dea is a fertility goddess known for her healing and restorative powers. Her name means "good goddess" and Roman women venerated her. Men were excluded from participating in her rituals and barred from entering her temples. Since her devotional practices were done in secret, not much is known about them. Still, they appear to have involved drinking wine, offering sacrifices, music, and dancing. Whether noble or enslaved, all women were welcomed to participate in her rituals.

Bona Dea was worshipped in homes as well as in temples. Priestesses of Bona Dea ministered to the sick, and men were allowed to receive healing treatments, although not within the temples. Her feast days are December 4 and May 1. Snakes are considered sacred to this goddess, and gardens were tended in her honor.

Bona Dea can be called upon to assist with overall health and healing as well as with the release of bondage—whether physical, emotional, or the bondage of addiction.

If you'd like to connect with Bona Dea, here are some things to try:

- Celebrate life by dancing
- Listen to music that makes you feel joy
- Spend time gardening or strolling through a garden
- Use an image or figurine of a snake as a focal point for your meditation
- Give offerings to Bona Dea of wine and honey

Craft a personal petition to the Bona Dea. Below is an example for reference:

Good goddess Bona Dea, Matron of Rome, turn your loving gaze upon me. With a grateful heart for all the blessings I have already received, I respectfully ask that you assist me with all my healing endeavors. Please help me find the strength to release myself from the bondage of unhealthy relationships, addictions, and anything holding me back from receiving the gift of optimal health and happiness. Thank you. Thank you. Thank you.

Brahma (Deity, Hindu)

Brahma is the creator god of the Hindu pantheon, representative of the universe and all its contents.[5] Brahma is a supportive deity interested in the welfare of his creations, including humankind. Along with Vishnu and Shiva, he is a part of the Hindu trinity of principal deities. Brahma is depicted with four hands and four heads, each face pointing toward one of the four cardinal directions. Each hand holds a representation of Brahma's power. In one hand, he has the Vedas, sacred texts representing knowledge. Another hand holds a mala (a string of prayer beads) to show his connection to spirituality. A third hand holds a cooking instrument, representing holy fire. The fourth hand holds a pot of water, a symbol of creation and abundance. Brahma can be envisioned with a long white beard representing his sage-like wisdom and either seated on a lotus flower or riding upon a swan.

Brahma can provide support for profound healing of body, mind, and spirit. He can help with transforming any area of your life and increasing abundance.

To align with the powerful energies of Brahma, consider the following activities:

- Meditate upon a statue or image of Brahma
- Chant *Sat Chid Ekam Brahma* (pronounced "saht cheed eh-kahm Brah-mah"). This mantra is traditionally chanted 108 times for a period of forty days; however, this practice can be modified to suit your needs.
- Give an offering of incense
- Read sacred texts such as the Upanishads and the Vedas

Here's one example of a personal petition to Brahma:

Great and Mighty Brahma, I respectfully request your guidance and support. Please assist me in finding the knowledge and re-

---

5. Thomas Ashley-Farrand, *Healing Mantras: Using Sound Affirmations for Personal Power, Creativity, and Healing* (New York: Wellspring Books, 1999), 222.

sources to help me on my journey toward greater health and wellness. Help me to create the conditions to achieve my healing goals. I open myself up to receive the gifts of an abundance of love, happiness, and inner peace. With a grateful heart, I give you thanks. Thank you. Thank you. Thank you.

Brighid (Deity, Irish; Saint; Ascended Master)

Brighid is the great goddess of Ireland, Keeper of the Sacred Flame. She is a fiery sun goddess, at times a warrior, and at other times a loving protector, depending upon the situation. Brighid is often depicted with three faces, representing different facets of her personality. Additionally, she can also be thought of as a shape-shifter, able to take on the form that best reflects the needs of her devotees. She holds dominion over healing, poetry, music, metalworking, and prophecy. She is also responsible for the arts, education, and livestock. Brighid is often depicted with flaming red hair in the company of a white cow and, occasionally, with a wreath of serpents on her head.

As Catholicism spread through Europe, Brighid was transformed into Saint Bridgit of Kildare. Brighid's feast day is celebrated on Imbolc (February 1 or 2), and bonfires were lit to mark the celebrations. Additionally, Brighid is considered an Ascended Master who can be called upon to access your own inner fire for transformation and personal growth.

Brighid can be called upon to assist with overall healing, healing after sexual abuse, fertility issues, healing of children, confidence, depression, empowerment, and courage.

Here are some suggestions for connecting to the Brighid's dynamic energies:

- Sit before a campfire or other fire source and appreciate the dancing of the flickering flames
- Draw or create a Brighid's cross. Alternatively, you can purchase a Brighid's cross and hang it in your home or office.
- Give an offering to Brigid, such as ale, blackberries, or coins

- Engage in artistic practices
- Meditate with crystals such as fire agate, carnelian, or Connemara marble

Compose a personal petition to Brighid. What follows is a sample:

O great goddess Brighid, Keeper of the Sacred Flame, please hear my call. It is my heartfelt intention to form a relationship with you and work with your powerful healing energies. Please assist me in becoming a powerful healer so I can effectively heal myself and share the gift of healing with others. Please help me find the courage needed to face the challenges ahead. Ignite my inner flame, and let me shine my light with confidence. Thank you. Thank you. Thank you.

Carna (Deity, Roman)

Carna is a Roman goddess of the physical body and healing. Carna's energy is one of protection as she shields those in need from spiritual assaults and physical illness. She is also associated with carnal pleasures and sensuality. According to legend, the god Janus, who has dominion over doors, gates, and transitions, was so captivated by Carna that he changed her into Cardea, the goddess of hinges, so she would always be close to him.

Carna can be called upon for physical healing, especially related to digestion issues, absorption of nutrients, healing the internal organs, and eating disorders, as well as protection from physical and spiritual attacks.

To align with the healing and protective energies of the goddess Carna, consider the options below:

- Pay attention to your diet, especially your food's quality and nutritional value
- Make offerings to Carna of fava beans or flour made of ground fava beans
- Show appreciation for your physical body by getting a massage or taking a restorative bath

Here's an example petition to Carna:

O powerful goddess Carna, please hear these words and answer my call. With a respectful and grateful heart, I ask for your assistance in healing my physical body, improving my capacity to absorb the nutrients needed to assist with this healing, and providing me with the strength to face any and all challenges. Also, please provide me with spiritual healing, helping me absorb the spiritual sustenance that fuels my soul. Grant me your protection physically and spiritually from today through my last day. Thank you. Thank you. Thank you.

Cernunnos (Deity, Celtic)

Cernunnos is an ancient Celtic deity whose name is typically translated as *"The Horned One."* Cernunnos is depicted with a man's body and a stag's horns. He often carries a bag of coins or grain and holds a cornucopia, the horn of plenty. The oldest surviving image of Cernunnos was found in the Italian Alps and is dated to the fourth century BCE. Representations of Cernnunos can be found throughout Europe. He is associated with nature, animals, the underworld, abundance, and healing. He is also associated with the Wild Hunt, in which the spirits of the dead are escorted to the Otherworld.[6]

Cernunnos can help with physical healing, forming a deep connection to Mother Earth, ancestral healing, healing of pets and animals, anxiety, stress, and assisting with the process of death and dying.

To explore the powerful energies of Cernunnos, consider the following activities:

- Meditate outside, preferably while sitting directly on the ground or a rock
- Spend time walking or hiking in nature
- Explore a cave or cavern
- Donate to animal-related causes or charities

---

6. R. J. Stewart, *Celtic Gods, Celtic Goddesses* (London: Cassell Illustrated, 1992), 4.

Develop a personal petition to Cernunnos. Here's one example:

Cernunnos, Horned One, I come to you requesting your blessings and favor. As my body is made from the elements of earth, I ask for profound healing of my physical body to restore me to optimal health. Increase my vitality and strength so that I can live a productive and meaningful life in harmony with all beings. I am grateful for your assistance in helping me reach my healing goals. Thank you. Thank you. Thank you.

Chiron (Deity, Greek)

Chiron is a mythological creature known as a centaur, with a man's torso and a horse's hindquarters. The animal portion of the centaur represents humankind's animal instincts, while the human part depicts humankind's higher nature, illustrating our dual nature as humans. Centaurs are typically depicted as uncivilized beasts, but Chiron is an exception. Chiron was educated by the sun god, Apollo, and studied the healing arts among other subjects.

Chiron became an adept healer and was Asclepius's primary teacher. Chiron later sacrificed his own mortality to save Prometheus, the bringer of fire to humankind, from Zeus's punishment. After spending nine days in the underworld, Chiron was immortalized in the constellation Sagittarius.

Known as the Wounded Healer, Chiron is a generous spirit and a patient teacher who can be called to assist with all types of healing: physical, mental, emotional, spiritual, and energetic. He can also help healers to strengthen and hone their healing abilities.

To connect with the healing energies of Chiron, consider trying the following suggestions:

- Read myths and legends about Chiron
- Star gaze and appreciate your place in the universe
- Meditate on an image of Chiron

Here's a sample personal petition to Chiron:

I call to the Wounded Healer, Chiron, forever immortalized in the stars. I am on a journey of healing and personal transformation. I am ready to learn about the healing arts and humbly request that you be my teacher and guide. Please guide me on the best wellness practices I can incorporate into my life to reach my healing goals. Thank you. Thank you. Thank you.

Coventina (Deity, British)

Often depicted as a mermaid, Coventina is a British goddess of bodies of water, including rivers, springs, wells, ponds, and oceans. She is known for her assistance with healing, fertility, prophecy, inspiration, and abundance. Coins and jewelry were thrown into her sacred well as offerings for her blessings, which may be the origin of the wishing well tradition. As a water deity, Coventina is known to connect to her devotees through the watery depths of the subconscious mind through dreams. Veneration of Coventina spread throughout Britain and the Celtic regions of Europe, Roman territories, and as far as Spain.

Coventina can assist with general health, emotional healing, fertility issues, relationship issues, depression, anxiety, the flexibility of body and mind, body-image issues, strengthening your intuition, and abundance.

To align with the healing energies of the goddess Coventina, consider these options:

- Place an image or statue of a mermaid on an altar dedicated to Coventina. Consider drawing, painting, or sculpting the image yourself for a more powerful experience.
- Give offerings to Coventina, such as spring water, coins, or jewelry
- Take a sacred bath with essential oils, flowers, or herbs. During the bath, ask Coventina to purify and heal you.

- Spend time near bodies of water such as oceans, lakes, or streams
- Connect with Coventina in your dreams by writing down your healing requests and placing the letter under your pillow as you sleep

The following is a sample personal petition to Coventina:

Goddess Coventina of the purest water, please turn your loving gaze upon me. Pour your soothing waters over me, revitalizing my body, heart, and mind. Please wash away negative thoughts and habits preventing me from reaching my healing goals. Please heal my wounded heart and mend my broken relationships. For your presence in my life, I am eternally grateful. Thank you. Thank you. Thank you.

Diana (Deity, Roman)

Diana is a commanding moon goddess of the Roman pantheon, equated with the Greek Artemis. Her mythology begins with her birth, which was said to be painless for her mother. Immediately after her own birth, she assisted her mother with the birth of her twin brother, Apollo. She precedes over magic, fertility, the wilderness, animals, women, and children. Hers is an independent spirit associated with outlaws and outcasts who often took refuge in the forest where she dwelled and hunted. Diana has an affinity for wild animals, especially dogs, wolves, and deer.

Diana can assist with childbirth, pregnancy, the healing of animals, self-confidence, physical fitness, independence, establishing boundaries, and developing inner strength.

To connect with the powerful energies of the goddess Diana, try the following activities:

- Give offerings that may include oak leaves, wine, and cakes
- Spend time in nature, especially forests or heavily wooded areas
- Bathe in the moonlight

- Meditate with crystals such as moonstone, amethyst, or blue chalcedony

If you'd like, compose a personal petition to Diana. Here's one example:

Goddess Diana, Luminous One, please hear my call. Please shine your light upon me and share with me your powerful energy. Please help me develop the inner strength and fortitude to stand in my personal power. Enhance my ability to be my authentic self and shine my light in the world. Thank you. Thank you. Thank you.

Demeter (Deity, Greek)

Demeter is the Corn Mother, the powerful Greek goddess of agriculture, the harvest, the seasons, and parenthood. In ancient Greece, it was she who taught humanity the secrets of agriculture, and her most popular myth involves the abduction of her daughter Persephone by Hades, the god of the underworld. In her grief, Demeter prevented crops from growing as she wandered, looking for her lost daughter. Eventually, a bargain was struck, and Persephone could spend half the year with her mother and the remainder of the year in the underworld.

Demeter is a shape-shifting goddess who may materialize in many forms, including a beautiful, mature woman with golden wheat-like hair, a horse, or a crone. She is often depicted as a triple goddess, along with Persephone and Hecate. She may appear holding wheat, poppies, doves, or alongside dolphins.

Demeter can provide support for all types of healing, healing parent-child relationships, self-care, grief, depression, inner strength, and living in harmony with nature.

To connect with the nurturing energies of Demeter, consider the following activities:

- Give offerings of wheat, bread, or pomegranates
- Set up an altar for Demeter with tokens relating to her myth, such as sheathes of wheat, a cornucopia, or figurines or images of pigs, horses, grasshoppers, and snakes

- Read the Orphic Hymn dedicated to Demeter, number 40
- Meditate with moss agate, red jasper, or petrified wood crystals

Here's a sample personal petition to Demeter:

Demeter, Corn Mother, please hear my call and turn your compassionate gaze my way. You who have provided nurturing and sustenance to the earth, please assist me in finding the support I need for optimal health and well-being. Please help me to nourish my body, mind, and spirit. Please assist me in finding the strength and courage to face any and all hardships that I may encounter along my healing journey. With a grateful heart, I give you thanks. Thank you. Thank you. Thank you.

Dhanvantari (Deity, Hindu)

As the celestial physician of the gods, Dhanvantari is a Hindu deity believed to be an incarnation of Vishnu. Emerging from the ocean of milk with a jar of the divine nectar of immortality for the demigods, Dhanvantari is credited with sharing the gift of Ayurveda, a holistic system of medicine, with humanity. His purpose is to assist with alleviating the suffering of humanity. Dhanvantari can be pictured as an attractive man with four hands; one or two of the hands hold a jar of amrita, the elixir of immortality. Alternatively, he may carry a book of Ayurveda, herbs, or a conch shell.

Dhanvantari can be called upon for healing blessings of all kinds, including chronic illnesses, protection during surgery, finding appropriate medical care and accurate diagnosis, as well as learning about holistic healing treatments.

If you'd like to explore the energies of Dhanvantari, try the following:

- Recite the Vedic mantra associated with Dhanvantari: *Om Sri Dhanvantre Namaha* (pronounced "aum shree don-von-trey nah-mah-hah") translated as "Salutations to the being and power of the Celestial Physician"[7]

- Meditate upon an image of Dhanvantari
- Learn about the holistic practices of Ayurveda

The following is a sample petition to Dhanvantari:

I call upon the Celestial Physician, Dhanvantari. Please hear my humble request made with a grateful heart for all the blessings I have already received. Destroyer of illness and disease, please assist me in my deep healing quest. Please make available to me the tools, resources, and knowledge I need to achieve my healing goals. Please supply me with guidance, encouragement, and strength so I can reach optimal health and great happiness. Thank you. Thank you. Thank you.

Durga (Deity, Hindu)

Durga is a powerful goddess of the Hindu pantheon. According to her mythology, she was created by the Hindu gods Vishnu, Shiva, and Brahma to defeat the fearsome demons attempting to conquer the etheric realms. She is a ferocious warrior and an independent goddess often depicted riding upon a lion or tiger. Durga can be visualized as a beautiful woman adorned with jewels and possessing ten arms, some holding powerful items: a conch for happiness, a trident for courage, an arrow and bow representing character, a club for loyalty, a sword for discrimination, and a chakra for righteousness.

Durga can assist with health issues and remove the causes of suffering. She can protect all levels of your being: physical, mental, emotional, and spiritual. Durga can assist with financial health and fertility. Additionally, she can help you stand in your personal power and enhance your courage and strength.

---

7. Ashley-Farrand, *Healing Mantras*, 115.

If you'd like to align with the protective and healing energies of the goddess Durga, try the following:

- Give offerings of flowers, mangoes, or incense
- Meditate upon Durga's yantra, a specific geometric pattern aligned with her associated energies
- Plant marigolds or place marigolds in a prominent place in your home
- Meditate with crystals such as tiger's eye, hematite, or obsidian

Here's a sample personal petition to Durga:

Durga, Invincible One, you who eliminates suffering, I come to you seeking your blessings. I ask for your wisdom and protection. Help alleviate suffering in all areas of my life. Please provide me with great healing on all levels of my being. Please help me to stand in my personal power, finding the courage and strength to face any adversity. Please favor me with an abundance of good health today and all my days. Thank you. Thank you. Thank you.

Eir (Deity, Norse)

Eir is a Norse goddess of healing and a Valkyrie, one of the mythical female escorts of deceased Nordic warriors to Valhalla. On the battlefield, she has the power to both heal the wounded and resurrect the dead. Eir is also reported to be a handmaiden to the goddess Frigg, the queen of Asgard and wife of the god Odin. She is often pictured on a hill surrounded by helping spirit allies.

Eir is associated with herbology, the study of herbs for medicinal purposes and magical healing. In addition, she has an affinity with shamanism and energy healing and is willing to assist those who also practice these arts. Eir can also help with overall healing, depression, anxiety, vitality, strength, and courage.

If you'd like to align with the energies of the goddess Eir, try one of the following activities:

- Sit on a hill in contemplation, imagining yourself surrounded by divine spirit healing guides
- Meditate on the colors associated with Eir—blue, green, red, and purple
- Read the Poetic Edda, an epic poem depicting stories of the Norse gods, goddesses, and heroes
- Make offerings to Eir of beer, wine, fruit, or herbs
- Grow or purchase white flowers for your altar or home

Here's a sample petition to Eir:

O powerful goddess Eir of the Valkyries, please assist me as I focus on my goals of greater health and happiness. Please help me to find the strength and courage to face any challenges I encounter along the way. With a respectful and grateful heart, I ask that you share your healing energies and wealth of healing knowledge with me. Thank you. Thank you. Thank you.

Francis of Assisi (Saint)

Francis of Assisi was born to a wealthy family on September 26, 1181. After an intense spiritual experience, he turned his back on his affluent lifestyle and embraced the path of a simple monk. He is credited with founding the Franciscans, a religious order within the Catholic Church.

After taking a vow of poverty, he ministered to the sick and dying. In 1224, Saint Francis of Assisi displayed the wounds of the stigmata, the injuries Jesus Christ suffered during the crucifixion. Saint Francis of Assisi died of natural causes in 1228. Two years after his death, he was canonized as a saint by Pope Gregory IX. His feast day is October 4.

Saint Francis of Assisi can be called up to assist with the healing and protection of animals, healing of families and family relationships, overall health, inner peace, connection to the Divine, assistance with the process of death and dying, and the healing of the planet.

If you'd like to develop a connection with the healing energies of Saint Francis of Assisi, try the following practices:

- Meditate on a picture or statue of St. Francis of Assisi
- Burn a brown candle every day for nine consecutive days
- Recite the prayer of Saint Francis of Assisi
- Engage in an activity to help heal the planet, such as picking up trash from a local street or beach
- Donate to a charity that supports the healing of the environment or your local animal shelter

Here's a sample personal petition to Saint Francis of Assisi:

Saint Francis of Assisi, Patriarch of the Poor, adorer of all animals, great and small. Please grant me peace and strength during this difficult time. Please fill me with divine love and bring peace into my heart. Please assist with deep healing on all layers and all levels of my being so I may live a productive life and be of service to others. Thank you. Thank you. Thank you.

Frejya (Deity, Norse)

Frejya is one of the most beloved goddesses of the Norse pantheon. Her father, Njord, is the god of the sea, and her mother, Herta, is the goddess of the earth. As a fertility goddess, Frejya rules over birth and death as well as the domain of Folkvang, where her palace holds the souls of departed warriors. Freyja is also the goddess of love, sex, pleasure, and magic. Freyja is known to be a shape-shifter but can be envisioned as a beautiful woman who has long, golden hair and is wearing an amber necklace and a cloak made of feathers. She is often depicted riding upon a chariot pulled by two cats.

Frejya can assist with fertility issues, healing of romantic relationships, problems connecting to sensuality or sexuality, low self-esteem, body-image issues, and understanding personal needs.

If you'd like to develop a connection to the kindhearted energies of the goddess Frejya, you could try the following:

- Connect with your sensual side through movement, physical touch, or by taking a luxurious bath with essential oils like jasmine, geranium, lavender, ylang-ylang, or rose
- Write a poem dedicated to Frejya
- Play music for Frejya that makes your heart joyful
- Provide offerings to Frejya, which may include honey, flowers, or apples
- Meditate with crystals connected to the energies of Frejya, such as amber, labradorite, or pearls

Here's a sample personal petition to Frejya:

Goddess Freyja, She Who Shines Over the Sea, I ask that you come to me today to assist me along my path of healing and personal transformation. Please bring more love into my life, heal my relationships, and help me connect with my sensual nature. I am ready to nurture myself and actively participate in my own self-care. Please provide me with your favor, ensuring that I will successfully fulfill all of these desires. Thank you. Thank you. Thank you.

Gabriel (Archangel)

Archangel Gabriel is one of the most prominent and beloved angels of Christian lore as well as the Islamic and Jewish faiths. Archangel Gabriel's name means "Hero of God" or "God is my strength" in Hebrew. Archangel Gabriel may be envisioned wearing blue robes and holding a lily, symbolizing peace. Additionally, Archangel Gabriel is associated with the element of water, the direction of the west, and the season of autumn.

Archangel Gabriel makes numerous appearances throughout the Bible, but perhaps the most famous is the visitation to Mary to announce that she was pregnant with the son of God. In the Catholic tradition, Gabriel is regarded as a Catholic saint with a feast day on March 24.

Archangel Gabriel can be called upon to assist with emotional health, pregnancy, fertility problems, children's health issues, anger issues, grief, depression, relationship problems, and overall healing.

To align with the healing energies of Archangel Gabriel, consider the following practices:

- Listen to the sound of falling rain or a waterfall
- Spend time connecting to Archangel Gabriel's element, water, by taking a soothing bath or spending time near a body of water
- Place lilies, the flower of Archangel Gabriel, in a prominent place in your home
- Watch a sunset with appreciation

Here's a sample of a personal petition to Archangel Gabriel:

Archangel Gabriel, Hero of God, please hear my heartfelt plea. I ask for your divine assistance in bringing peace into my body, my mind, and my heart. With your healing chalice, pour purifying waters over me, gently washing away anything not in alignment with my greatest good. Please help heal my relationships, soothe my wounded heart, and improve my overall health and well-being. Thank you. Thank you. Thank you.

Gaia (Deity, Greek; Ascended Master)

Gaia is the great earth mother of Greek mythology. She *is* the earth, not separate from it. Gaia materialized directly from the primordial chaos and created the sky, the seas, mountains, lakes, and all organic life, including humans. Gaia is the mother of the predecessors to the gods, the titans, who ruled the heavens and earth before being overthrown by Zeus and his siblings.

Gaia is also the spirit of honor, justice, and integrity. Oaths and promises were sworn in Gaia's name, and temples and shrines were built in her honor. The priestesses at Delphi invoked Gaia as primordial earth mother as part of their divination rituals. Additionally, Gaia is considered an Ascended Master who can be called upon to assist with your connection to the earth.

Gaia has tremendous compassion for humanity and can assist with all types of healing: physical, emotional, mental, and spiritual. Additionally, she can help with healing parent-child relationships, fertility issues, depression, anxiety, and the ability to manifest your inner vision into this material plane.

To align with the nurturing and supportive energies of Gaia, try the following activities:

- Give offerings to Gaia of honey and pure water. These offerings can be made directly on the soil.
- Donate to an environmental cause
- Plant a garden outside or a kitchen garden within your home
- Spend time walking, hiking, or exploring in nature
- Meditate with any of the following crystals: jasper, agate, petrified wood, or aventurine

Here's a sample personal petition to Gaia:

Gaia, Great Mother, I have embarked on a journey of healing and personal growth. As the earth constantly evolves, I, too, am evolving. I invite your nurturing energies to sustain me during this challenging time. Help heal my body, mind, and soul. Allow me to form a deep connection with the earth and receive the assistance needed to manifest my inner vision of perfect health into reality. Thank you. Thank you. Thank you.

Ganesha (Deity, Hindu)

The much-beloved and elephant-headed Hindu god Ganesha is the son of Shiva, the essence of the divine masculine, and Parvati, the essence of the divine feminine. There are many myths associated with Ganesha. One of the most popular is the story of the race around the universe. There was a contest to see which deity would be honored first during ceremonies. Shiva and Parvati issued this challenge, stating that whoever circled the universe three times would receive the award of being honored first during ceremonies and before any new undertakings. Deities proceeded to their mounts as the challenge began. Disappointed, Ganesha headed toward his mount, a rat, knowing that he wouldn't stand a chance against deities who had faster mounts like eagles or peacocks. As he contemplated his plight, the answer dawned on Ganesha. He rode his rat around his mother, Parvati, three times and won the contest. How? Parvati, the Divine Mother, *was* the universe, and her body was the divine energy of the cosmos in the illusion of forms.[8] As a result, Ganesha is always the first deity venerated in all ceremonies and provides successful outcomes when invoked before new ventures.

As the lord of new beginnings, Ganesha can assist you as you start any new endeavor, including a new fitness routine, diet or nutrition plan, job, or relationship. Ganesha can remove any obstacles, including obstacles preventing you from achieving your goals for greater health and happiness. Ganesha can facilitate healing on all levels—physical, emotional, mental, and spiritual. Ganesha can also assist with financial health and abundance.

To connect with the supportive and healing energies of Ganesha, consider the following practices:

- Meditate upon an image or statue of Ganesha
- Give offerings of fruits and sweet treats
- Chant *Gum*, the seed (bija) mantra associated with Ganesha. This mantra is traditionally chanted 108 times for a period of forty days; however, this practice can be modified to suit your needs.

Here's a sample personal petition to Ganesha:

---

8. Thomas Ashley-Farrand, *Chakra Mantras: Liberate Your Spiritual Genius Through Chanting* (San Francisco: Red Wheel/Weiser, 2006), 85.

*Dearest Ganesha, Removers of Obstacles and Lord of Blessings, I
come to you with a pure heart seeking your favor. As I embark on
this new healing journey, I ask for your blessings for this new chapter of my life to be successful. Please remove everything preventing me from achieving my goals of greater health and happiness.
Please provide me with financial abundance so I can easily support
myself and my family. For all you do, I give you thanks. Thank you.
Thank you. Thank you.*

Gemma Galgani (Saint)

On March 12, 1878, Saint Gemma Galgani was born near Lucca, Italy,
to a middle-class Italian family. By the time she was seven years old, her
family had suffered the loss of her mother to tuberculosis, and she was
sixteen when she also lost her brother, Gino, to the same disease. Her father died of cancer when Gemma was nineteen. Feeling a calling to serve
God by joining the Passionist covenant as a nun, her plans were placed
on hold when she developed a series of life-changing diseases, including
losing her hearing due to meningitis, scoliosis, sores on her head, and
depression. However, Gemma continued her devotional practices and was
restored to perfect health. In 1899, she began to display stigmata (the crucifixion wounds of Jesus), and she reported mystical experiences of visions
of Jesus Christ and Mother Mary. Saint Gemma also described seeing and
communicating with her guardian angel. She died in 1899 from tuberculosis and was canonized as a saint on May 2, 1940. Her feast days are April
11 and May 16.

Saint Gemma can be called up to aid with physical and mental healing, assistance with disabilities, depression, and anxiety, and deepening
your connection with both angels and the Divine.

To develop a connection with the healing energies of Saint Gemma,
try one or more of the following activities:

- Give offerings of roses or lilies
- Meditate on an image of Saint Gemma
- Donate to a charity that supports individuals with disabilities

Compose a personal petition to Saint Gemma, such as the following:

Saint Gemma, Daughter of the Passion, I am drawn to you and your communication with the angelic realms. Please help me to establish an intimate connection with angels and communicate with these blessed beings of love and light. Please assist me on my path toward greater health and wellness. Please open my heart to the Divine and aid my spiritual growth and development. Thank you. Thank you. Thank you.

Gnomes (Elemental)

Gnomes are the elementals associated with the earth element, which is traditionally related to the direction of the north as well as the winter season. The characteristics of the earth element include the physical body, stability, structure, dependability, groundedness, and financial resources.

Gnomes can assist us with deepening our connection to the earth element and embodying characteristics associated with it. The gnomes can be imagined in various sizes but are typically smaller than the average human. They are traditionally dressed in the colors of the earth, including browns and greens. Typically, gnomes are quiet and reserved in nature but enjoy receiving gifts. The gnomes are governed by a monarch named Ghob, who stands as tall as a human, with a long white beard and a compassionate but aged face.

Healing with the earth element and the gnomes can assist with healing the physical body, achieving a grounded state, protection, good luck, reduction of stress and anxiety, and achieving financial health.

To attune to the grounding energies of the gnomes, consider the following activities:

- Meditate outdoors, preferably seated directly on the ground and facing north
- Give some gifts or tokens, such as crystals and sweet treats
- Mindfully walk barefoot on the grass or the soil

- Cultivate the earth by growing a flower or vegetable garden
- Read myths, fairy tales, and folktales about the earth elementals, the gnomes, and other types of earth nature spirits, such as elves and trolls
- Donate to an environmental cause or animal sanctuary

If you'd like to craft a personal petition, here is one to Ghob, the monarch of the gnomes:

Dearest Ghob, Monarch of the Gnomes. Please teach me how to live as a worthy steward of this fantastic planet. Please help me to connect deeply with the energies of the earth element. Please assist me with obtaining greater physical health and a reduction of the stresses of modern living. Please provide me with the resources I need to achieve greater financial stability. I am grateful for your presence in my life. Thank you. Thank you. Thank you.

The Green Man (Nature Spirit)

The Green Man is the personification of nature. He represents the persistent nature of life itself. The Green Man is a symbolic representation of rebirth as represented by the season of spring, when new life springs forth after the long winter months. He also portrays the eventual deterioration of matter back to earth, represented by the season of fall. The Green Man symbolizes fertility, vitality, and libido.

The Green Man is a common motif whose image can be seen in architecture, Gothic churches, graveyards, and outdoor shrines. He is depicted as a male head composed of foliage crowned with leaves. An alternative form of the Green Man is a male head with a "beard" of vegetation.

The Green Man can assist with vitality, protection, connection with nature, anxiety and stress, depression, sexual dysfunctions, and fertility issues.

To develop a connection with the regenerative energies of the Green Man, consider the following practices:

- Meditate upon an image of the Green Man
- Create an outdoor garden
- Show your appreciation for the earth by recycling, picking up litter, or donating to an environmental cause
- Meditate with a crystal associated with the energies of the Green Man, such as moss agate, petrified wood, green jasper, or green obsidian

Here's a sample personal petition to the Green Man:

O Green Man, Ancient One, you who are the personification of nature, please hear my simple request. Help me release any burdens that are currently preventing me from reaching my goals of greater health and well-being. I ask that these worries be released to the earth, where they can be transmuted into positive energies that can assist me along my life path. Please increase my vitality, strength, and connection to the earth so I can be a beacon of light to others. Thank you. Thank you. Thank you.

Gula (Deity, Mesopotamian)

Gula is the Mesopotamian goddess of healing in the Mesopotamian pantheon. She not only possessed the ability to cure diseases but also caused illness when provoked or angered. According to her mythology, Gula rescued humanity after the Great Flood. She is often depicted seated on a throne accompanied by a dog. Her home is a sacred garden located in the center of the world, where she waters the tree that forms the world's axis. In addition, Gula is known for her knowledge of herbs for healing purposes.

Gula is a wise and compassionate goddess. She can assist with overall health, self-care, fertility issues, pregnancy, stress, anxiety, depression, and the knowledge of plants for medicinal purposes.

To bond with the healing energies of Gula, consider the following activities:

- Meditate in a garden or with a flower as the focal point of your meditation
- Donate to a charity focused on assisting animals, especially dogs
- Learn about the healing benefits of plants

Craft a personal petition to Gula, such as the following:

Gula, goddess of medicine, hear my call. Please act as my divine physician, curing all my health-related issues and restoring me to perfect health. As you water and nurture the tree that forms the world's axis, please nurture me, encouraging me to engage in more self-care practices. Please assist me with reducing the stress and anxiety that plague my daily life and keep me from enjoying life's simple pleasures. With a grateful heart, I give you thanks. Thank you. Thank you. Thank you.

Haniel (Archangel)

Archangel Haniel is an approachable angel who is always ready to assist when called upon. According to Thomas Heywood's 1635 book *The Hierarchy of the Blessed Angels*, Archangel Haniel is one of the seven great archangels.[9] In Hebrew, Archangel Haniel's name means "Glory" or "Grace of God" or "He who sees God." Archangel Haniel may be envisioned wearing seafoam-green robes.

Although not explicitly mentioned in the Bible, Archangel Haniel is thought to be the angel who accompanied Enoch to Heaven. Archangel Haniel is associated with *Netzach*, the seventh sphere on the Kabalistic Tree of Life, and the planet Venus, which is connected with love and beauty.

Archangel Haniel can be called upon to assist with relationship issues, matters of the heart, enhancing creativity, cultivating more joy in daily life, connecting with your sensual nature, and developing healing abilities.

---

9. Gustav Davidson, *A Dictionary of Angels Including the Fallen Angels* (New York: The Free Press, 1971), 134.

To align yourself with the healing energies of Archangel Haniel, try one or more of the following:

- Place roses (a flower connected to Haniel's Venusian energies) in a prominent place in your home
- Engage in creative practices, such as painting, drawing, poetry, pottery, and so on
- Spend quality time with loved ones

Here's a sample personal petition to Archangel Haniel:

Archangel Haniel, Grace of God, I come to you with an open heart to ask for your divine assistance. Please help me attract peace, joy, and harmony in all aspects of my life. Please have the energy of pure love flow effortlessly into my being. May I be healed and my natural healing abilities amplified. Thank you. Thank you. Thank you.

Hathor (Deity, Egyptian)

One of Egypt's most beloved goddesses, Hathor, was revered for more than three thousand years as the goddess of love, abundance, music, the underworld, and the sky. Hathor may translate to "House of Horus," which is appropriate as Hathor is the mother (and perhaps wife) of the sky god, Horus. In her role as mother, she acts as a healing goddess and protector. In mythology, she is said to have miraculously restored Horus's eyesight after an injury. She often appears as a woman with a crown composed of a solar disk flanked by two cow's horns. An alternative depiction of Hathor is a woman with the ears of a cow. However, Hathor is a shape-shifter who may manifest as a cow, cat, falcon, hippopotamus, cobra, and lioness.

Hathor can assist with issues of health, protection of any type, cultivating more joy in life, abundance, self-care, and problems with fertility and pregnancy, as well as the process of death and dying.

To align with the healing and protective energies of the goddess Hathor, you could try the following:

- Give the traditional offering of two mirrors
- Wear jewelry associated with Hathor, such as turquoise or malachite
- Spend time listening to music or dancing
- Meditate on a statue or image of Hathor

Here's a sample personal petition to Hathor:

Hathor, Great One of Many Names, I come to you seeking your blessings. I ask for your guidance and protection. As you restored Horus's eyesight, please restore me to a state of perfect health. Please help me embrace a life filled with joy, love, and good fortune. Please favor me with an abundance of good health and happiness, today and all my days. Thank you. Thank you. Thank you.

Hecate (Deity, Asia Minor)

Hecate, Queen of the Night, is a goddess whose origins are lost to time but may have been in Asia Minor. Her name may be a feminine version of the masculine *Hekatos,* "worker from afar."[10] She has many titles and epithets, providing insight into her many roles in ancient myths: Light-Bringer, Key-Holder, the One Before the Gate, and Most Lovely One.

Hecate is a shape-shifter appearing as a maiden, various animals, and a triple-headed figure with heads of a serpent, horse, and dog. Alternatively, she can be envisioned as a young woman in saffron robes, crowned with oak leaves. She has an affinity with the wilderness, graveyards, and animals, especially dogs. She travels through the heavens, the underworld, and upon the earth.

Hecate is a powerful but benevolent deity who can assist with healing, protection, victory in any conflict, self-confidence, standing in your personal power, and granting wishes.

---

10. Sorita d'Este, *Circle for Hekate–Volume I: History & Mythology* (London: Avalonia Books, 2017), 34.

To connect with the powerful energies of the goddess Hecate, consider the options below:

- Give offerings to Hecate, such as hard-boiled eggs with honey, pomegranates, incense, or spring water
- Spend time bathing in the moonlight
- Wear or carry a key as a symbol of your connection to Hecate
- Read the Orphic Hymn to Hecate (number 1)
- Donate to a local animal shelter, especially one that cares for dogs

Here's a sample personal petition to Hecate:

Hecate, Queen of the Night and the Crossroads, please hear my words. Help me take action and choose the path that aligns with my highest potential and assist me in reaching my healing goals. Unlock the gates that bar me from obtaining health and happiness. Please provide me with protection, today and all of my days. I am grateful for your presence in my life and your assistance. Thank you. Thank you. Thank you.

Heka (Deity, Egyptian)

Heka is the Egyptian god of magic, healing, and medicine. For the ancient Egyptians, *heka* (magic) was a divine force that existed in the universe, similar to strength and power.[11] Thus, Heka the deity was considered the personification of magic itself. He is often depicted as a man holding two serpents but is sometimes portrayed as a divine child. Heka accompanied the sun god Ra on his solar barge in its daily voyage across the sky, protecting the barge as it traversed the underworld during the night. Since the ancient Egyptians associated magic with healing, doctors and healers of ancient Egypt were frequently called priests of Heka.

---

11. Richard H. Wilkinson, *The Complete Gods and Goddesses of Ancient Egypt* (London: Thames & Hudson, 2017), 110.

Heka can assist with any type of healing: physical, emotional, mental, and spiritual. He can also help with protection and the development of magical abilities.

To develop a connection with the healing and magical energies of Heka, you could try one or more of the following activities:

- Perceive and appreciate the magic in daily life
- Burn incense of frankincense or myrrh
- Meditate on an image of Heka

Here's a sample personal petition to Heka:

Heka, mighty god of magic and healing, please turn your gaze upon me. Please awaken the magical force of healing energies within me, restoring my vitality and energy so I reach a state of optimal health. Please grant me your protection, physically, mentally, emotionally, and spiritually, today and every day. Thank you. Thank you. Thank you.

Hilarion (Ascended Master)

Hilarion is an Ascended Master dedicated to healing humanity and the planet. He is reported to have lived many lifetimes, including as a healer in Atlantis and ancient Egypt. In one lifetime, he lived in Syria during the fourth century CE. During this lifetime, he converted from paganism to Christianity and dedicated his life to spiritual development. After the death of his parents, he donated his inheritance to his siblings and others in need. He then retreated to live a life of seclusion and prayer in a cave.

Hilarion can be called upon to assist with all types of healing: physical, mental, emotional, and spiritual. He can also help establish boundaries, prioritize self-care, heal relationships, and strengthen your connection to the Divine. If you are an energy healing or medical professional, Hilarion can act as a teacher, improving your healing abilities and knowledge of the healing arts.

To form a connection to the healing energies of Hilarion, try the following:

- Burn a green-colored candle in honor of Hilarion
- Spend time walking or meditating in a cave
- Connect with your emotions through journaling, reading poetry, or listening to music that makes your heart sing
- Donate to a local charity focused on helping those experiencing financial hardships
- Meditate with green crystals such as emerald, green jasper, and malachite

Here's a sample personal petition to Hilarion:

Great Hilarion, I have embarked on a journey toward greater health and well-being and call upon you to assist me with this endeavor. Please assist me in connecting to the Divine, filling my heart with pure love. Please help me to establish the boundaries needed to protect my emotional and energetic health. Please restore me to perfect health, giving me the vitality and energy to serve others in need. I am grateful for your assistance and your presence in my life. Thank you. Thank you. Thank you.

Hygeia (Deity, Greek)

Hygeia, the ancient Greek goddess of health and healing, is the daughter of the mythical divine healer Asclepius. Hygeia may work with her father but is not a lesser or subordinate divine being. Her name is the basis for the word *hygiene,* which denotes cleanliness and is the basis of good health. Her primary focus is on preventive medicine and the protection of good health.

Hygeia has an affinity for snakes and is often pictured as an attractive young woman wearing long robes with an enormous snake wrapped around her body or arm. She is also connected with the moon and lunar healing energies, which have been said to aid mental health ailments.

Hygeia can assist with issues of health, preservation of health, mental health concerns, and preventive medicine.

To develop a rapport with the healing energies of Hygeia, try the following practices:

- Make a traditional offering to Hygeia of hair, clothing, pieces of fabric, fruit, wine, and incense
- Meditation with a crystal associated with Hygeia, including moonstone, clear quartz crystal, or amethyst
- Take a leisurely bath with sea salt and embrace her love of cleanliness
- Soak in the moonlight and connect with its healing powers
- Read the Orphic Hymn to Hygeia (number 68)

Here's a sample personal petition to Hygeia:

Goddess Hygeia, daughter of Asclepius, I humbly seek your guidance and counsel. As the goddess of health and wellness, please share your healing knowledge with me so that I may gain insights to assist with my own healing and help others with their healing process. Please protect my current health as I work toward my healing goals. Please guide me on what preventive measures I can take now so that I may enjoy good health in the future. I am grateful for your participation in my healing journey. Thank you. Thank you. Thank you.

Itzamna (Deity, Maya)

Itzamna is the powerful Maya god of medicine and is credited for establishing the ancient Maya empire that flourished throughout the Mesoamerican region from approximately 250 BCE to 1697 CE. As the lord of both the night and the day, he displayed his wisdom of the cycles of creation by developing the famous Maya calendar. Itzamna's gifts to his people include maize, a staple of the diet in this region, and cacao, a tasty bean with healing properties. Known for his peaceful nature, Itzamna is the patron of healers and writers. He is usually depicted as a wise and mature man.

Itzamna is an approachable god who takes an interest in individuals actively engaged in their own healing process. He can assist with physical and emotional healing, depression, anxiety, stress management, cultivating more peace in life, and using plants for medicinal purposes.

To develop a connection to the healing energies of Itzamna, try one or more of the following activities:

- Tamales are one of Itzamna's favored offerings; enjoy eating a tamale in Itzamna's honor or make an offering of one
- Write a poem or short story dedicated to Itzamna
- Develop your intuition or divination skills
- Create an altar to Itzamna with tokens such as obsidian stones or figurines of lizards and fish

Here's a sample personal petition to Itzamna:

Mighty and wise Itzamna, god of healing, I call to you. With your knowledge of the cycles of life, please help me connect with my own natural rhythms to facilitate great healing, both physical and emotional. I am ready to release anything holding me back from achieving optimal health and peace in my heart. I respectfully request your assistance in achieving these goals. With a grateful heart for your participation in my journey toward greater health and happiness, I give you thanks. Thank you. Thank you. Thank you.

Imhotep (Deity, Egyptian)

Imhotep inspired a rich mythology as an important official of the Egyptian third dynasty. He is credited with overseeing the construction of the incredible step pyramid at Saqqara, generally considered the first Egyptian pyramid. Although born a human, his accomplishments and dedication to the god Ptah inspired the legend that he was the son of Ptah, born to a mortal woman. In addition to his accomplishments as an architect, he was also known for his intellectual pursuits and was dubbed the patron of medicine. Imhotep is often illustrated as a man holding an open papyrus scroll, a symbol of his academic achievements.

People seeking healing would pray and sleep in temples dedicated to Imhotep, hoping that he would visit them in their dreams with healing advice or remedies for their illnesses. Some travelers to the temples of Imhotep would also leave representations of their illness or diseased body parts with the hope that Imhotep would heal these afflictions.

Imhotep can assist with any healing: physical, emotional, mental, and spiritual. He can also help with learning disabilities, ADHD, anxiety, depression, inner peace, and connection to the dream world.

If you'd like to align with the healing energies of Imhotep, try one or more of the following:

- Record your dreams in a dream journal to connect to the healing power of dreams
- Burn frankincense or myrrh incense
- Meditate on an image of Imhotep
- Engage in intellectual pursuits, such as reading or puzzles
- Decorate your home or office with pyramid-shaped crystals

Here's a sample personal petition to Imhotep:

Great Imhotep, builder of the step pyramid of Saqqara, seeker of knowledge, I humbly request your guidance and sage insights. Please give me the wisdom to make the necessary changes in my life so I may live in perfect health and harmony. Please bless me with peace both in my mind and in my heart. Please facilitate healing on all layers and at all levels of my being so I may live a productive life and be of service to others. I am grateful for your contributions to achieving my goals of greater health and happiness. Thank you. Thank you. Thank you.

Inanna (Deity, Mesopotamian)

Inanna is an ancient Mesopotamian goddess with several epithets and titles: Queen of the Heavens, Lady of Victory, the One Who Is Joy, and Lady of the Sky, among others. Inanna is known as the goddess of both war and love, a hint of her dual nature. Inanna's cult in the ancient world was widespread, and she became such an important goddess that she assimilated most of the other ancient Sumerian goddesses.

Many myths featuring Inanna are documented in Sumerian literature. Her myths include her travels into the underworld, where she was taken prisoner until the trickster god Enki rescued her. Inanna is also credited with giving the tablets of destiny to humanity, prompting the birth of civilization. Additionally, her many amorous adventures depict her connection with both sensuality and sexuality, as well as female sexual empowerment.

Inanna can assist with a host of issues, including restoration of health, protection, strength, abundance—including financial abundance, good fortune, connection to sexuality, female empowerment, healing from sexual trauma, healing of romantic relationships, and the transition from life to death.

If you'd like to develop a connection to Inanna, try one or more of the following practices:

- Make an offering of figs and wine
- Create an altar for Inanna with figurines or images of animals associated with her, such as lions, snakes, dolphins, hedgehogs, and doves
- Embrace your sensual nature through dance, dressing in luxurious clothing, holding hands with a loved one, receiving a massage, or soaking in a bath with essential oils such as jasmine or ylang-ylang
- Meditate with crystals associated with the energies of Inanna, such as lapis lazuli, orange calcite, and jade

Here's a sample personal petition to Inanna:

Goddess Inanna, Lady of Victory, I ask that you come today not as a warrior goddess but as a powerful deity of healing and love. As the goddess of healing and destruction, please provide me with relief from my current afflictions of body, mind, and heart, destroying anything that is holding me back from reaching a state of optimal health and happiness. Please assist me in standing in my personal power and facing adversity with strength and courage. Please help me achieve my goals of greater health and happiness. Thank you. Thank you. Thank you.

Isis (Deity, Egyptian; Ascended Master)

Isis, Queen of the Throne and Mistress of Magic, is one of the Egyptian pantheon's most widely revered goddesses. Over thousands of years, her popularity extended beyond Egypt to include portions of Asia and Europe. Some of ancient Egypt's best-known myths include stories of Isis, including her resurrection of her husband/brother, Osiris, and her powerful capacity for performing high magic. She is a shape-shifter who may take the form of a cow, kite (a bird of prey), or even a scorpion. Isis is portrayed in many forms: a seated woman nursing a child, a beautiful woman with wings, wearing a crown garnished with a throne or a crown containing a crescent moon between two horns. She is associated with both the moon and the constellation Virgo. Additionally, Isis is considered an Ascended Master who can assist you with reclaiming your personal magic.

Isis is a benevolent, approachable, and powerful goddess. She can assist with all types of healing, pregnancy, marital issues, self-esteem, connection to the divine feminine, strength, protection, and magic.

If you'd like to bond with Isis's dynamic energies, try one or more of the following practices:

- Meditate on a statue or image of Isis
- Diffuse essential oils associated with Isis, such as myrrh and vervain

- Give offerings such as flowers, milk, or honey
- Bathe in the moonlight
- Look for the magic in everyday experiences
- Meditate with crystals associated with the energies of Isis, such as carnelian, lapis lazuli, turquoise, amethyst, and green jasper

Here's a sample personal petition to Isis:

Isis, Queen of the Throne, please embrace me with your loving wings and hear my request. Please help me gain confidence and strength that enable me to face life's challenges. I would like your assistance in teaching me to harness the powers of healing so I can be restored to perfect health and be of service to others. Please bestow upon me your protection, today and all of my days. With an open and loving heart, I give you thanks. Thank you. Thank you. Thank you.

Ixchel (Deity, Maya)

Ixchel is a Maya goddess ruling over healing, fertility, creativity, childbirth, and sex. According to her mythology, Ixchel fell in love with the sun, which angered her grandfather, who responded by murdering her in a jealous rage. For thirteen days, dragonflies mourned over her place of burial until she came back to life and rejoined the sun to be lovers. Unfortunately, over time, the sun became jealous of her relationship with her brother, the morning star. To cope with the sun's behavior, Ixchel made herself invisible whenever the sun ventured near her and found sanctuary in rainbows.

Ixchel is a triple goddess with a maiden, mother, and crone manifestation. She is both a compassionate, nurturing goddess and a destructive force. When associated with fertility, she is often depicted with her companion, a human-sized rabbit. When associated with her more aggressive side, Ixchel may appear as an elderly woman holding a water jug that can release hurricanes and torrential rains.

Ixchel can assist with various issues, including overall health, fertility issues, pregnancy and childbirth, healing from family trauma, removing creative blocks, and healing emotional wounds.

To connect with the healing energies of Ixchel, try one or more of the following activities:

- Create a simple altar with tokens for Ixchel. You could include objects such as crystals, figurines of dragonflies, rabbits, snakes, spiders, sea shells, and rainbows.
- Take a restorative bath with sea salts and essential oils
- Place rainbows in prominent areas of your home
- Spend time near a body of water such as the ocean, a lake, or a stream
- Meditate with crystals associated with the energies of Ixchel, such as rainbow moonstone, opal, rainbow fluorite, and moon quartz

Here's a sample personal petition to Ixchel:

Ixchel, Lady of the Rainbow, I call upon you with an open heart. I ask for your intervention and assistance in radically transforming my life into one full of health, happiness, and abundance. Please help me heal all my relationships. Please help me release childhood traumas and open my heart to forgive those who hurt me through both words and actions. Please help me find my personal rainbow, my sanctuary, and grant me the knowledge, skills, and wisdom to serve others. With a grateful heart, I give you thanks. Thank you. Thank you. Thank you.

Jesus of Nazareth (Deity; Ascended Master)

Jesus of Nazareth is also known as Jesus Christ. The story of Jesus's life can be found in the four Gospels of the New Testament of the Bible. Although the Gospels were written long after Jesus's death, they provide an account of the life of Jesus from different points of view. Attributed to Matthew, Mark, Luke, and John, all four agree on the central theme that Jesus is the divine savior of humankind who taught lessons of love, forgiveness, and peace. Moreover, the New Testament is filled with stories of miracles, including acts of physical and mental healing Jesus had performed. In the New Age movement, Jesus is regarded as an Ascended Master whose message of love and healing transcends religious dogma.

Jesus can assist with the healing of all aspects of your life, including physical, mental, emotional, and spiritual healing. In addition, Jesus can provide divine guidance, support, and protection. He can also be called upon to assist with the healing of relationships and finances, facilitating forgiveness, and performing miracles when your situation appears hopeless.

If you'd like to explore Jesus's loving and supportive energies, consider trying the following:

- Meditate upon an image or statue of Jesus
- Read stories of Jesus's life, such as those in the Bible
- Consciously practice forgiveness in your life
- Donate money or volunteer at a charity that assists people experiencing poverty, such as in a soup kitchen or a food pantry
- Volunteer your time at a local charity

Develop a personal petition to Jesus, such as the following:

Jesus, Lamb of God, please hear my words. I ask for your divine intervention in my life. I open my heart to you and your energies of love and peace. Please teach me how to forgive others as well as forgive myself; love others as well as love myself; be at peace with others as well as find my own inner peace. Grant me the blessings of health and well-being so I can live my life to my fullest potential and serve others. Thank you. Thank you. Thank you.

Jizo (Bodhisattva)

Jizo, whose name translates to *Womb of the Earth* or *Earth Treasure*, is a compassionate and loving bodhisattva. Jizo specifically is Japanese, but this figure is also known as Ksitrigarbha in Sanskrit and Dayuang Dizang in Chinese, among others. Jizo has gained popularity and followers in his own right and may be considered a separate spiritual being.

Jizo has a particular affinity for children, acting as both a guardian and healer. He is said to protect the souls of unborn babies as well as children who have died before their parents. In addition, he protects living children and aids in their recovery from illness and disease.

Jizo's potential for offering help isn't limited to children, although that is his specialty. He can assist everyone with all types of healing: physical, emotional, mental, and spiritual. Jizo can also help with fertility issues, pregnancy, childbirth, depression, anxiety, overall health, protection from evil, enlightenment, forgiveness, and success in any endeavor.

To connect with Jizo's healing and protective energies, consider the following:

- Place a statue of Jizo in a prominent place in your home
- If you request protection or healing for a specific child, attach a small piece of the child's clothing or red cloth to a statue of Jizo
- Practice random acts of kindness
- Donate to causes that are dedicated to the welfare of children

If you'd like to compose a personal petition to Jizo, here's an example:

Jizo, Earth Treasure, hear my humble request. I wish to form a relationship with you and ask for your blessings. Please assist me with my own journey of healing, granting me greater health and well-being. I also ask that you provide deep healing and lasting protection for my child, who also needs your aid. Please grant me success in all my healing goals. Thank you. Thank you. Thank you.

John of God (Saint)

John of God was born João Duarte Cidade in Portugal on March 8, 1495, to a poor religious couple. It is reported that when John was just a child, he was abducted by a mysterious stranger and lived with a family in Spain who raised him as their own child. John's path in life was complicated; he became a mercenary soldier and was eventually dishonorably discharged from service.

His life was transformed during his travels in the Pyrenees when he encountered a solitary child. John picked up and carried this child along a rocky mountain road. Upon reaching a spring, John set the young boy down and drank from the waters. When he turned back to the boy, the boy had transformed into a divine child who presented John with a pomegranate crowned with a cross. This child instructed John to change his name to "John of God" and to go to Granada. The divine child disappeared, leaving John to follow the instructions.

In Granada, John founded a hospital that ministered to the poor, which survived after his death in 1572. Those who worked in his hospital declared themselves a religious order known as the Brothers of Saint John of God or sometimes the Brothers Hospitallers. It is this order that is now responsible for the health care of the Pope. On October 16, 1690, Pope Alexander VIII canonized John of God, and his feast day is March 8.

As a saint, John of God can be called upon to assist with overall healing, mental health issues and addictions, as well as support for healthcare providers and healers.

To align with the energies of St. John of God, try one or more of the following:

- Donate to a charity focused on assisting the disadvantaged
- Give offerings of pomegranates and water
- Meditate on an image of the sacred heart

Here's a sample of a personal petition to St. John of God:

Saint John of God, I call to you with an open and loving heart. As you transformed your life, please assist me in radically transforming my life into one of health and happiness. I humbly ask that you be my advocate in my healing process and my protector against disease and illness. Please assist me with restoring my body, mind, and spirit to optimal health as well as alleviating the suffering of all those in need. Thank you. Thank you. Thank you.

Jophiel (Archangel)

Archangel Jophiel is a friendly angel with an uplifting, supportive energy whose name means "Beauty of God." Archangel Jophiel may be envisioned wearing purple or magenta robes. Although not explicitly mentioned in the Bible, Archangel Jophiel is thought to be the angel who escorted Adam and Eve out of Eden after they ate the apple from the Tree of Knowledge.

Archangel Jophiel is considered the patron angel of the arts. Working with Archangel Jophiel can help you attract more beauty and creativity into your life. Archangel Jophiel can be called upon to assist with depression and sadness, heal body-image issues, find beauty in any situation, and enhance creativity.

To connect with the uplifting energies of Archangel Jophiel, try one or more of the following:

- Light a purple candle in honor of Archangel Jophiel
- Spend time in a park or garden
- Appreciate the beauty in the ordinary

Here's a sample personal petition to Archangel Jophiel:

Archangel Jophiel, Beautiful One, Patron of the Arts, I come to you with an open mind and a grateful heart, seeking your assistance. Please help me see and appreciate the beauty in myself and ordinary, everyday experiences. Please have your creative energies flow effortlessly into my being, assisting with finding innovative solutions to problems in my life that need to be fixed. Please lift all sadness from my heart and fill my days with joy. Thank you. Thank you. Thank you.

Joseph (Saint)

Joseph, the husband of Mother Mary, is the adoptive father of Jesus Christ. He is described in the Bible as a carpenter who taught this craft to his son, Jesus, and is the patron saint of workers. Although the Bible doesn't reveal much of Joseph's life, it is believed that he passed away in the company of both Jesus and Mother Mary, leading Pope Pius IX to declare him the patron of the sick and for a contented death as well as the protector of the Catholic Church.

Joseph is known for his compassion and readiness to assist all those who call upon him. According to a Sicilian legend, Saint Joseph was asked to monitor the gates of Heaven while Saint Peter attended to other matters. Instead of selectively admitting entrants into Heaven, Saint Joseph let everyone inside. Needless to say, Saint Peter was quickly called back to resume his duties!

Saint Joseph can assist with issues relating to paternity, father-child relationships, healing of family relationships, marital healing, finding meaningful employment, financial healing, and issues regarding housing or finding a suitable home.

If you'd like to connect with the compassionate and industrious energies of Joseph, try one or more of the following:

- Light a green or yellow candle in honor of Saint Joseph
- Give Saint Joseph offerings of incense, lilies, or keys
- Meditate upon a statue or an image of Saint Joseph
- Volunteer or donate to a food pantry

Here's a sample personal petition to Saint Joseph:

Saint Joseph, please turn your benevolent gaze upon me. I come to you in a time of need. Please assist me in the healing of all my relationships—especially with my children and with my spouse (if applicable). Please help me to be compassionate, patient, and kind. Please help me to forgive those who have wronged me. Aid me in all my endeavors, including greater financial health and stability, as well as my desire to be of service to others. Thank you. Thank you. Thank you.

Jude Thaddeus (Saint)

Saint Jude is believed to be Judas Thaddeus, a companion of Jesus Christ and one of the twelve apostles, not to be confused with Judas Iscariot, the betrayer of Jesus before his crucifixion, as is written in the Bible. During his lifetime, Judas Thaddeus performed healings and exorcisms. He is called the Miraculous Saint, the patron of lost and desperate causes. He is eager to assist with even the most hopeless of causes. He can be envisioned wearing green robes adorned with a sacred medal on his chest with flames above his head, representing the presence of the Holy Spirit. His feast days are October 28 in the Roman Catholic Church and June 19 in the Eastern Orthodox Church.

Saint Jude can be called upon for any and all requests, including (but not limited to) physical healing, financial health, healing of relationships, stress, anxiety, and depression.

If you'd like to connect with the supportive energies of Saint Jude, try one or more of the following:

- Practice random acts of kindness
- Each day for nine days, place fresh basil in a small vase or bowl of water before a statue or image of St. Jude
- Donate to your favorite charity
- Light a green novena candle in honor of St. Jude
- Meditate holding chrysoprase, a crystal associated with St. Jude

Here's a sample personal petition to Saint Jude:

O Blessed Saint Jude, Patron of Lost Causes, please hear my petition made with a sincere heart. Please walk with me on my life journey and facilitate healing on all levels of my being: physical, mental, emotional, and spiritual. Please stand by my side during the challenges in my life. With your assistance, may hopelessness be transformed into optimism, positivity, and joy. May peace live forever in my heart and throughout the world. Thank you. Thank you. Thank you.

Kwan Yin (Deity, Chinese; Bodhisattva; Ascended Master)

Kwan Yin is a compassionate, loving goddess and a beloved figure in Buddhist traditions. Kwan Yin is also known as Guanyin, the Chinese name for the Sanskrit *Avalokiteśvara*, which translates to *The one who responds to the cries of the world*.[12] Originally, Avalokiteśvara was an androgynous or male figure considered the manifestation of the Buddha Amitabha. However, in Korea, Japan, and China, this deity transformed into her current female manifestation.

Kwan Yin is considered a bodhisattva, an enlightened being who chose to remain in human form, assisting humanity rather than ascending to nirvana. Although Kwan Yin is revered in Buddhism and other traditions, her influence extends beyond the constraints of any single religion. She is also considered an Ascended Master, and her message of compassion and mercy transcends religious dogma.

Kwan Yin can assist with deep healing on all levels of your being, including fertility issues, depression, anxiety, body-image issues, healing for children and animals, financial health, finding joy in life, self-love, compassion for both yourself and others, protection, good luck, enlightenment, and strengthening your spirituality.

To connect with the compassionate and healing energies of Kwan Yin, try one or more of the following:

- Meditate upon a statue or image of Kwan Yin
- Give offerings of incense, oranges, and pomegranates
- Read the Lotus Sutra
- Practice random acts of kindness

---

12. Judika Illes, *The Encyclopedia of Mystics, Saints & Sages: A Guide to Asking for Protection, Wealth, Happiness, and Everything Else!* (New York: HarperCollins, 2011), 413.

- Chant the Sanskrit mantra *Om Mani Padme Hum* (pronounced "aum mah-nee pahd-may hoom"). Mantras are traditionally recited 108 times for forty days, but feel free to modify this practice as needed.

Here's a sample personal petition to Kwan Yin:

Kwan Yin, Mother of Compassion, please hear my request. In this time of personal turmoil, I come to you with an open and loving heart. Please assist me with profound physical, emotional, mental, and spiritual healing. Please bring more joy and tranquility into my daily life. Please show me how to access a greater capacity for compassion and love so that I can be a beacon of light and love for others. Please protect me, today and all of my days. With a grateful heart, I give you thanks. Thank you. Thank you. Thank you.

Lady Nada (Ascended Master)

Lady Nada is an Ascended Master and part of the Council of Light whose goal is to awaken humanity to Christ Consciousness, the personal awareness of unity with the Divine and spiritual bliss. Lady Nada's vocation is to guide humanity toward embodying the expression of divine love. She is reported to have previous incarnations as a priestess of Atlantis and other ancient civilizations. Lady Nada is connected with the heart chakra, the energy center associated with love and compassion. Lady Nada can be envisioned as a beautiful golden woman wearing pink robes and holding a rose.

Lady Nada can assist with forgiveness, self-love, body-image issues, connection to divine love, emotional healing, problems concerning fears and phobias, as well as healing relationships of any kind.

To align with the loving and healing energies of Lady Nada, try one or more of the following:

- Light a pink candle in her honor
- Read poetry or listen to music that connects with you emotionally

- Wear pink or rose-colored clothing or jewelry associated with the energies of Lady Nada
- Write a love letter to yourself
- Meditate with a crystal associated with the energies of Lady Nada such as rose quartz, pink chalcedony, or kunzite

Here's a sample personal petition to Lady Nada:

Dear Lady Nada, I wish to align myself with your loving energies. Please help strengthen my emotional body and heal my wounded heart. Please assist me in forgiving others unconditionally and for-giving myself for all my past mistakes. Please fill me with divine love so I can be a beacon of love and light to others. With a grate-ful heart for your presence in my life, I give you thanks. Thank you. Thank you. Thank you.

Lalita (Deity, Hindu)

Lalita is the Hindu goddess of love and a personification of feminine beauty. Her myths also reveal her strength when she battles the danger-ous and evil demon, Bhanda, a creation of the ashes of Kama, the god of pleasure and desire whom Shiva destroyed for the offense of disrupting his meditation. When Lalita defeated the demon, she also restored Kama to life, bringing back pleasure and desire; however, these attributes were now under Lalita's control.

Lalita can appear as a beautiful young woman with delicate features, a loving smile, four hands holding a noose, a spiked stick used for driv-ing cattle, a bow, and five arrows made of flowers. She is often depicted sitting upon a lotus resting upon a bed supported by her consort, Sa-dashiva, and the legs of the bed are formed by four male deities. This image is a symbol of her status as a supreme power, worshipped even by those who govern the cosmos itself.[13]

---

13. Sally Kempton, *Awakening Shakti: The Transformative Power of the Goddess of Yoga* (Boulder, CO: Sounds True, 2013), 282.

Lalita is a loving and nurturing goddess. She can assist with overall health, connecting to the feminine aspects of yourself and your sensuality, healing from sexual trauma or sexual issues, healing relationships, success, and abundance.

To align with Lalita's loving and sensual energies, try one or more of the following activities:

- Light a red candle in Lalita's honor
- Use Lalita's yantra (a geometric image) as a focal point of your meditation
- Recite the seed (bija) mantra *hrim* (pronounced "hreem"). Mantras are traditionally recited 108 times over forty days, but feel free to modify this practice as needed.
- Explore your feminine nature through creative acts such as dance, writing, or painting
- Explore your sensual side by taking a luxurious bath, massage, or lovemaking

Here's a sample personal petition to Lalita:

Lalita, Goddess of Love and Desire, I call to you with a loving heart. Shine your brilliant light upon me, infusing my being with your energies of love and happiness. Please assist me with healing the feminine parts of myself, those aspects I have neglected for too long. Please help me appreciate my body and practice the self-care I need. Please give me the strength to overcome any challenges I may face and succeed in all my endeavors. Fill me with your love so that I may share it with others. With a grateful heart, I give you thanks. Thank you. Thank you. Thank you.

Lakshmi (Deity, Hindu)

Lakshmi is the goddess of abundance, wealth, beauty, and joy. She is a compassionate deity willing to assist anyone who calls upon her with love and gratitude. According to the Mahabharata, an epic poem written in

Sanskrit, Lakshmi emerged from the churning ocean of milk as a beautiful, youthful woman adorned in white garments whom all the gods desired. She selected the god Vishnu and became his wife and loving companion. She is depicted as standing or sitting upon a large lotus flower, a symbol of enlightenment. She may be envisioned dressed in a pink sari and is often accompanied by two painted elephants.

Lakshmi can assist with abundance in all forms, including an abundance of health, relationship healing, self-love, fertility issues, self-confidence, good fortune, joy, and financial health.

To bond with the loving energies of Lakshmi, try one or more of the following:

- Meditate on a statue or image of Lakshmi
- Light a pink candle in her honor
- Grow holy basil, an herb associated with Lakshmi
- Give offerings such as flowers, fruit, coins, or sweet treats
- Recite the seed (bija) mantra *shrim* (pronounced "shreem"). Mantras are traditionally recited 108 times over forty days, but feel free to modify this practice as needed.

Write a personal petition to Lakshmi such as the following:

Lakshmi, Beautiful Lady of Good Fortune and Abundance, please turn your loving gaze upon me and accompany me on my journey of healing and personal growth. Fill me with your loving energy, healing my wounded heart and expanding my ability to love others as well as myself. I respectfully ask for your blessings of an abundance of good health and good fortune. With a joyful heart for your presence in my life, I give you thanks. Thank you. Thank you. Thank you.

Mae Thorani (Deity, Thai)

Mae Thorani is a popular Buddhist deity revered in Thailand. She protects the earth and all humans who live upon it. She is described as a beautiful, young, dark-skinned woman with blue eyes and long green hair that reaches the earth. According to her mythology, when Gautama Buddha was meditating under the bodhi tree, he was attacked by the demon Mara and his army, determined to stop the Buddha from reaching enlightenment. Mae Thorani sprang forth from the earth and wrung out her lengthy hair, soaked with the waters of libations offered to the Buddha over the years. The torrent of water from her hair flooded the area, driving Mara and his army away. The Buddha then proceeded to attain enlightenment.

Mae Thorani can assist with all types of protection: physical, mental, emotional, and spiritual. She is also a powerful ally to help with fertility issues, addictions, and compulsive behaviors. She can also assist with grounding, reduction of stress and anxiety, and cultivating inner peace.

If you'd like to connect with the protective and healing energies of Mae Thorani, try one or more of the following:

- Light a green candle in her honor
- Diffuse blue lotus essential oil, which is associated with Mae Thorani
- Give offerings of pure water, flowers, rice, or sugar cane
- Spend time in nature connecting to the earth

Here's a sample personal petition to Mae Thorani:

Dearest Mae Thorani, I come to you in my time of need. Please cloak me in your protection, shielding me from all harm, be it physical, mental, emotional, or spiritual. Please help me to slay my inner demons, providing me with inner peace and harmony. Thank you for your presence in my life and on my journey toward greater health and happiness. Thank you. Thank you. Thank you.

Maeve (Deity, Irish)

Maeve is an ancient Irish warrior goddess of sovereignty. She was a kingmaker called upon by rulers as they assumed power for her blessings of strength and prosperity. Known for her intoxicating beauty as well as her strength, she rode into battles on her chariot and decimated armies. She was not only a goddess of war and death but also fertility, sex, and abundance. She is an independent goddess who embraces her sexuality and epitomizes feminine beauty.

After the spread of Christianity, Maeve was transformed into a fae queen, sometimes referred to as Mab, a miniature version of her warrior persona. She can be envisioned as a beautiful woman wearing a gown of red or green with a bird on her right shoulder and a squirrel on her left.

Maeve can assist with physical healing relating to menstrual cycles, fertility, body-image issues, and sexual dysfunction. She can also help you connect to your inner power, reclaim your sovereignty, and provide you the strength to reach your healing goals. Knowledge about alternative medicines and herbology is also under her purview.

If you'd like to synchronize with Maeve's energies, consider the following activities:

- Walk upon grassy green hills reminiscent of the hills of Ireland
- Light a red candle in her honor
- Create a simple altar dedicated to Maeve with images of rainbows, flowers, and figurines of birds and squirrels
- Read plays or fairy tales featuring Maeve or Mab
- Meditate with crystals such as moss agate, rainbow fluorite, and garnet

Here's a sample personal petition to Maeve:

Maeve, Goddess and Queen of Old, please hear my words and answer my requests. Your balance of both warrior and feminine energies inspires me. I am ready to stand in my power and take charge of my healing journey. Please give me the strength and vitality to reach all my healing goals and overcome obstacles. Help me appreciate my physical body and embrace my sensual nature. I am

grateful, Fairy Queen, for your presence in my life. Thank you.
Thank you. Thank you.

Mami Wata (Deity, Western and Central Africa)

Mami Wata is a Western and Central African snake goddess and powerful water spirit who resided in a lake before emerging as an extremely
popular deity known throughout the modern world. She is known for
her zest for life, charismatic appeal, beauty, love of laughter, appreciation
for fine jewelry, and her ability to cause harm as well as heal. Mami Wata's
original depiction of a woman with the lower body of a snake has mor-
phed into her current portrayal as a mermaid. Additionally, she may be
visualized as a beautiful woman carrying expensive items such as combs
and jewelry. She is often portrayed holding or entwined with a snake and
holding a mirror, a symbol of movement from present to future.

Mami Wata can assist with various issues, including restoration of
health (especially when the causes of illness are unknown) and removing
fatigue, fertility issues, and sexual dysfunction. She may also grant the
blessing of abundance and financial health.

To align to the energies of Mami Wata, try one or more of the following practices:

- Make an offering to Mami Wata of lemonade, exotic fruits,
  and perfume
- Create an altar for Mami Wata with figurines or images of snakes
  and crocodiles
- Take a sacred bath with herbs and essential oils
- Meditate with azurite malachite or larimar crystals

Here's a sample personal petition to Mami Wata:

Dearest Mami Wata, Mother of Waters, the amazing snake god-
dess, please assist me with shedding all illness and lethargy within
my physical body. Revitalize my body, mind, and spirit so I can
live a full and meaningful life of happiness and love. Please bless

*me with success in all my endeavors, especially my goals of greater
health and well-being. Thank you. Thank you. Thank you.*

Manasa (Deity, Hindu)

Manasa is a Hindu serpentine goddess known as a naga. Nagas are mythological creatures who are half human and half cobra. Manasa, in particular, takes several different forms, including a snake or an alluring
woman surrounded by cobras. Manasa may appear with only one eye if
she reveals herself in female form. She is often depicted riding across the
sky in a chariot pulled by snakes or seated on a lotus flower.

Manasa is known to bestow many blessings, including healing, fertility, wealth, abundance, and success in all types of endeavors. As a
goddess of healing, she is mighty when battling infectious diseases and
removing poisons, especially snakebite venom. Manasa can also assist
with recovering from family trauma and rejection.

To connect to the healing energies of Manasa, try one or more of the
following:

- Place a small statue or image of a snake on an altar dedicated
  to Manasa
- Draw a picture of a lotus blossom or snake and use the image
  as the focal point of your meditations
- Diffuse lotus essential oil in the air
- Give Manasa offerings of flowers, fruits, milk, or incense
- Meditate with crystals aligned with Manasa's energies, such as
  serpentine and ammonite

Here's a sample personal petition to Manasa:

*O beautiful goddess Manasa, Goddess of Snakes and Remover of
Poisons, I come to you in a time of need. I wish to develop a relationship with you and work with your powerful healing energies.
As a remover of poisons, please help me by removing all toxins
from my life, including unhealthy relationships, negative thought*

patterns, and any toxins I may be unknowingly ingesting through my food or drink. Please assist me in becoming an effective healer of bodies, minds, and souls—not just for my personal benefit but for the benefit of others. Thank you. Thank you. Thank you.

Margaret of Castello (Saint)

Margaret of Castello was born to noble parents in Metola, Italy, in 1287. Unfortunately, she was born with severe disabilities that included blindness, curvature of the spine, and one leg being more than an inch shorter than the other. Her parents were embarrassed by her disfigurement and kept her isolated and hidden during her childhood. As a result of this neglect, she never grew taller than four feet.

Eventually, Margaret was abandoned by her parents but was cared for by a generous, loving couple who treated her as a daughter. Although Margaret's challenges would have turned many individuals toward bitterness, Margaret was intensely devoted to both God and helping others. This devotion inspired her to join the Third Order of St. Domenic, where she acted as nurse to the ill and ministered to the dying. She continued her work until she died in 1320 at the age of thirty-three. Miracles of healing have been attributed to Margaret, and she was canonized as a saint by Pope Francis on April 24, 2021. The feast day associated with Saint Margaret of Castello is April 13.

Saint Margaret of Castello can be called upon for anyone needing healing, especially those with physical deformities or disabilities. She can also provide healing and blessings to those who have been abandoned or rejected.

To bond with the loving energies of Saint Margaret of Castello, try one or more of the following:

- Light a white candle in her honor
- Spend time reading holy or inspirational texts
- Serve the disadvantaged and engage in works of charity

Here's a sample personal petition to Saint Margaret of Castello:

Saint Margaret of Castello, please hear this petition made with a true and faithful heart. I ask for your assistance in alleviating my suffering and transmuting my illness into health. Please help me receive deep healing for all layers of my being so that I can be a beacon of hope, love, and grace to others in need. Thank you. Thank you. Thank you.

Mary Magdalene (Saint; Ascended Master)

Mary Magdalene is one of the Bible's most prominent and recognizable women. She also played an essential role in many texts omitted from the Bible, such as the Gospel of Mary, discovered in Egypt in 1896. She has been portrayed in many roles, including a dedicated disciple of Jesus, a repentant prostitute, a "companion" of Jesus, and a sinner for whom Jesus exorcised seven demons. Although there isn't a consensus on who the historical Mary Magdalene actually was, her myth has transcended time. Mary Magdalene appears in the Arthurian legend, where she collects Jesus's blood in a chalice called the Holy Grail, and she is the protector of Jesus's blessed lineage. Additionally, Mary Magdalene is considered an Ascended Master whose message of forgiveness, strength, and confidence transcends religious dogma.

Mary Magdalene can assist with all types of healing: physical, mental, emotional, and spiritual. She can also be called upon to help with issues of forgiveness, faith, love, and your connection to the Divine.

If you'd like to connect with the compassionate energies of Mary Magdalene, try one or more of the following:

- Light a white candle in her honor
- Plant a rosebush or place roses in a prominent location in your home
- Diffuse essential oils associated with Mary Magdalene, such as spikenard or myrrh

- Meditate with crystals corresponding to Mary Magdalene's energies, such as alabaster, pink tourmaline, and black moonstone

Here's a sample personal petition to Mary Magdalene:

Dearest Mary Magdalene, cast your compassionate eyes in my direction. I wish to follow your example and embrace forgiveness, generosity, and love as a way of life. Please assist me with pursuing personal growth and deep healing on all levels of my being. Help me be a vessel for divine love and an example of love's power to inspire others. Thank you. Thank you. Thank you.

Maximón (Deity, Maya)

Maximón (pronounced "mah-shee-mon") is an ancient, compassionate Maya spirit. Many attempts have been made to merge him with the Christian saint Simon but have consistently failed. Instead, Maximón modernized his appearance, and his popularity spread through both the Americas and Europe. Known for his mischievous nature as well as his benevolence, Maximón is often pictured as a well-dressed man with a mustache, wearing a dark-colored suit and hat. He makes his existence known by appearing in dreams and as an unexplainable presence of the aroma of cigar smoke.

Maximón can be called upon to assist with all types of healing: physical, mental, emotional, and spiritual. He helps with recovery from addiction, both our own addictions and on behalf of someone unable or unwilling to ask for themselves. He can also assist with protection as well as financial health.

To form a connection to the benevolent energies of Maximón, try one or more of the following:

- Place an image of Maximón in your home or office
- Give offerings of carnations, tobacco products, silk scarves, tequila, soda, or hats

- Burn colored candles in honor of Maximón: pink for health, yellow for protection for adults, white for the protection of children, and green for prosperity

Here's a sample personal petition to Maximón:

Maximón, I come to you asking for your blessings and favor. Please assist me along my healing journey by restoring my body to perfect health. Please remove any addictive or compulsive behaviors preventing me from reaching my healing goals. Please wrap me in protective armor, shielding me from harm today and all my days. I am grateful for your assistance and your presence in my life. Thank you. Thank you. Thank you.

Medicine Buddha (Deity, Buddhist)

The Medicine Buddha's traditional Sanskrit name is *Bhaiṣajyaguru*, and is the aspect of the Buddha focused on healing, health, and medicine. There are twelve vows ascribed to the Medicine Buddha upon reaching the state of enlightenment that illustrate the ways in which the Medicine Buddha works toward relieving the suffering of humankind.

The Medicine Buddha is often depicted in a seated position wearing sacred robes and holding a lapis lazuli medicine jar in his left hand. His right hand gestures downward with the palm facing forward in a show of willingness to assist those in need and answer prayers. He can be envisioned surrounded by a rich blue aura, the color of lapis lazuli.

The Medicine Buddha can be called upon by anyone in need of physical, emotional, mental, energetic, or spiritual healing.

If you'd like to connect with the powerful healing energies of the Medicine Buddha, try one or more of the following:

- Meditate on the colors blue and gold, which are associated with the Medicine Buddha
- Meditate while holding a piece of lapis lazuli, or place this stone in a prominent area of your home

- Make an offering of fruit
- Read the Medicine Buddha Sutra, which is available in many places online
- Use an image or statue of the Medicine Buddha as a focal point for your meditation

Design a personal petition to the Medicine Buddha. Below is an example for your reference:

Wise, powerful, and compassionate Medicine Buddha, restorer of health and eliminator of pain, please shine your beams of brilliant light upon me during this challenging time. With an open and true heart, I ask that you assist me with all my healing endeavors. Please strengthen my physical body, restore my vitality, and fill me with peace. Please help me to walk a path in alignment with my divine purpose. Thank you. Thank you. Thank you.

Metatron (Archangel)

According to angelic lore, Archangel Metatron is the Old Testament prophet Enoch, who ascended and transfigured into a celestial being. Archangel Metatron plays an essential role as the scribe of the Book of Life, which documents the lives of all humans on Earth. Archangel Metatron may be visualized seated on a crystal throne wearing robes of brilliant white light.

Archangel Metatron is credited with leading the children of Israel out of the desert to safety during the Exodus and is particularly interested in children's welfare. In addition, Archangel Metatron is the angel assigned to the first sphere of the Tree of Life, Kether, representing unity with the Divine.

Archangel Metatron can be called upon to assist with guidance when making decisions, raising your personal vibration from a lower frequency to a higher one, the process of enlightenment, and the health and protection of children.

To align with the energies of Archangel Metatron, try one or more of the following:

- Read inspiring and spiritual books and poetry
- Develop a consistent meditation practice
- Contemplate images of sacred geometry, a favorite subject of Metatron

Here's a sample personal petition to Archangel Metatron:

Archangel Metatron, Chancellor of Heaven, please grant me your blessings. I ask for your assistance and intervention concerning the health and well-being of my child. Please guide the doctors, teachers, and all who come in contact with my child to add to his/her/their healing process. I ask for my own guidance so that I may be a beacon of light to my child and be divinely inspired to provide him/her/them with the tools and resources needed for growth and development. Finally, I ask that you protect my child now and always. Thank you. Thank you. Thank you.

Michael (Archangel)

Archangel Michael is one of the most recognized and most popular archangels of the Judeo-Christian tradition. This angel, whose name means "Who is like God?" in Hebrew, is a warrior angel often depicted wearing red robes and carrying a flaming sword. However, Archangel Michael has additional roles as protector, healer, and guardian. In addition, Archangel Michael is associated with the element of fire, the direction of south, and the summer season.

Archangel Michael has incredible gifts of healing and is responsible for the overall welfare of humanity. In Constantinople, he was considered the great heavenly physician. Pope Gregory credited Archangel Michael with ending the Plague of Justinian, which may have killed over one hundred million Europeans. Archangel Michael is also considered a Catholic Saint and has two feast days: May 8 and September 29, also called Michaelmas.

Archangel Michael can be called upon to assist with protection, increase energy and vitality, improve self-esteem, boost willpower, enhance passion, heal metabolism issues, provide strength and courage to battle disease, and improve overall health.

To connect with the powerful and energizing energies of Archangel Michael, try one or more of the following:

- Light a red candle in honor of Archangel Michael
- Meditate on the color red or incorporate more red-colored clothing into your wardrobe
- Engage in activities that ignite your inner fire or passion

Here's a sample personal petition to Archangel Michael:

Archangel Michael, I ask that your might be made merciful as I respectfully ask for your divine assistance. Please protect me on all levels of my being: physically, emotionally, mentally, and spiritually. Please enhance my vitality and strengthen my courage so that I can face any obstacles. Finally, please restore me to optimal health and improve my overall well-being. I am grateful for your assistance. Thank you. Thank you. Thank you.

Minerva (Deity, Roman)

Minerva is an ancient Roman goddess of Etruscan origin who was revered throughout the Roman Empire. Although Minerva has been equated with her Greek counterpart, Athena, these were initially two distinct goddesses. In her *Minerva Medica* persona, Minerva presides over the medical profession and healing arts.[14] Also a warrior goddess, Minerva is associated with craftsmanship and intellectual pursuits. Romans celebrated her feast day from March 19 to 23.

---

14. Judika Illes, *The Encyclopedia of Spirits: The Ultimate Guide to the Magic of Fairies, Genies, Demons, Ghosts, Gods & Goddesses* (New York: HarperCollins, 2009), 721.

Minerva can be envisioned as a physically fit, tall, attractive young woman wearing armor and carrying a spear. She is often accompanied by an owl, a symbol of knowledge and wisdom.

Minerva can assist with vitality, courage, mental clarity, intellectual development, learning disabilities, ADHD, stress reduction, physical healing, and mental health issues.

If you'd like to connect with Minerva's potent energies, try one or more of the following:

- Offerings of spring water, red wine, and olives
- Engage in intellectual pursuits such as solving puzzles and reading
- Explore a craft such as needlework, pottery, sewing, or stained glass
- Meditate on the image of the Queen of Spades playing card, which may serve as an image of Minerva

Here's a sample personal petition to Minerva:

Minerva Medica, I come to you with an open heart, requesting your blessing, power, and favor. May I receive the gifts of deep healing and robust health. May I receive your warrior power to fight any illnesses that may be present and for the courage to make the changes needed to improve my overall well-being. May I receive your favor to cultivate a state of inner peace and harmony. With a grateful heart, I give you thanks. Thank you. Thank you. Thank you.

Morya or El Morya (Ascended Master)

Morya (sometimes El Morya) is an Ascended Master and part of the Great White Brotherhood focused on humanity's spiritual evolution. He is reported to have lived multiple lifetimes, including past lives as King Arthur, Abraham, Sir Thomas Moore, and one of the three wise men who visited the infant Jesus, after his birth. Morya is connected with the throat chakra, the energy center associated with communication and speaking your authentic truth. Morya can be pictured as a wise man with electrifying blue eyes and a beard.

Morya can assist with overall healing—especially related to issues related to the throat or the ability to communicate effectively, establishing boundaries, strength, courage, energetic protection, and strengthening your spirituality.

To connect with the protective and strengthening energies of Morya, try one or more of the following:

- Light a blue or white candle in Morya's honor
- Explore your communication skills by writing poetry or an original short story
- Wear blue-colored clothing or jewelry to align with the energies of Morya and the throat chakra
- Meditate with a crystal associated with Morya, such as lapis lazuli, sapphire, or star sapphire

Here's a sample personal petition to Morya:

Morya, I am contacting you to establish a relationship and collaborate with you regarding my healing goals. I am a sensitive soul with an empathic nature. Please aid me in setting the boundaries I need to maintain my energetic and emotional health. Please help me to say no to activities and relationships that drain my energy. Please help me stand in my personal power and authentically speak my truth confidently. Please provide me with deep healing on all levels of my being: physical, mental, emotional, and spiritual. With a grateful heart for your presence in my life, I give you thanks. Thank you. Thank you. Thank you.

Mother Mary (Saint; Ascended Master)

Mother Mary, also known as the Virgin Mary, the Holy Mother, and Queen of Angels, among other titles, is the mother of Jesus. Although she is often categorized as a saint, she surpasses that classification. Among some devotees, dedication to Mary is just as strong as that to her son, Jesus Christ.

Details about Mary's life are described in the gospels. Born to a Jewish family, she married Joseph; however, before she had marital relations with her husband, the archangel Gabriel informed her that she was already pregnant with the Son of God, the Messiah. Mary was present during her son's spiritual leadership, and witnessed both the miracles he performed as well as his crucifixion.

Mary is known for her compassion, love, healing, and miracles. She is reported to have made appearances in various places, including Fatima in Portugal, Lourdes in France, Tepeyac Hill in Mexico City, and Medjugorje in Bosnia. Although Mother Mary is revered in Christianity, she is also considered an Ascended Master, and her message of love and compassion transcends any one religion.

Mother Mary provides aid to those in need, and her compassion knows no limit. She can assist with healing mother-child relationships and guidance regarding parenting. She can also help mothers who require healing for their children. She can assist with deep healing on physical, mental, emotional, and spiritual levels. She can also help allieviate depression, anxiety, and stress.

If you'd like to connect with the loving energies of Mother Mary, try one or more of the following:

- Light a blue candle in appreciation of Mother Mary
- Give Mother Mary offerings of incense, roses, lily of the valley, rosemary, or strawberries
- Meditate upon a statue or image of Mother Mary
- Donate your time or money to an organization that assists individuals experiencing poverty
- Recite the Hail Mary or Hail Holy Queen prayers

- Meditate with crystals associated with the energies of Mother Mary, such as blue lace agate, celestite, kunzite, selenite, pearl, and desert rose

Here's a sample personal petition to Mother Mary:

Blessed Mother Mary, Queen of Angels, cast your merciful eyes upon me and hear my humble request. Dearest Mother, I am in need of true healing. Please heal my physical body and restore me to optimal health. Please fill my heart with compassion, patience, and forgiveness so that I may be a more loving family member and friend. Let me live a life of joy, peace, and harmony so that I can be a beacon of light and love to others in need. Thank you. Thank you. Thank you.

Nana Buruku (Deity, West African)

Nana Buruku is a West African mother goddess of creation, healing, fertility, and victory. In the creation myth of many West African peoples, life sprang forth from a primeval swamp ruled by Nana Buruku. She is associated with swamps, wetlands, marshes, clay, and mud. She is a powerful force known for her harsh demeanor; however, she has great affection for healers, herbalists, and root doctors. She is known to assist with curing illnesses and diseases that have no known cause or treatment.

Nana Buruku can be envisioned as an elderly woman carrying a staff made from palm fronds and decorated with cowrie shells. A giant serpent may accompany her, or she may manifest in the form of a snake.

Nana Buruku can be called up for overall healing, fertility issues, depression, anxiety, stress reduction, knowledge of herbs for medicinal purposes, and using clay for healing purposes.

To connect to the powerful energies of Nana Buruku, you could try the following practices:

- Light a purple or lavender candle in Nana Buruku's honor
- Study and read books about herbalism

- Sculpt with clay
- Give Nana Buruku offerings of roses, cowrie shells, or roots, such as mandrake root
- Meditate with a tourmaline crystal, which is associated with Nana Buruku
- Hike or take a walk in a marsh or wetlands

Here's a sample personal petition to Nana Buruku:

Nana Buruku, Ancient and Wise One, Goddess of Swamps and Marshes, I come to you with an open heart and open mind. I wish to develop a relationship with you and work with your healing energies. I have an affinity for plants and herbs, and I ask that you act as my teacher, assisting me in learning herbalism as a healing modality. Please provide me deep healing on all levels of my being and protection today and all my days. Thank you. Thank you. Thank you.

Obatala or Oxala (Deity, Yoruban/West African)

Obatala, King of the White Cloth, is an orisha, a god of the pantheon belonging to the Yoruba people of West Africa, specifically southwestern Nigeria. He is the god of creation, healing, and peace. His legend says that the Supreme Creator gave him the responsibility for the creation of the earth. However, Obatala became intoxicated by overindulging in palm wine, which resulted in his deviating from the Supreme Creator's design for humanity. As a result, some humans were born with various disabilities and afflictions.

Obatala has a particular affinity with those with disabilities, both seen and unseen. He is a patient, compassionate deity who guides people to find peace, harmony, and justice. He presides over all things that are white, such as bones, silver, platinum, and white cloth. Obatala can be pictured with long white hair and wearing white robes.

Obatala can be called upon to assist with all types of healing, especially related to disabilities and congenital disabilities, healing after an argument, healing of bones or bone-related illnesses, releasing anger, issues related to fatherhood, inner peace, and cultivating patience.

To form a connection to the harmonious and healing energies of Obatala, try one or more of the following:

- Create your own peaceful oasis in an area of your home dedicated to promoting tranquility
- Give offerings of milk, white rice, coconuts, white sugar, or white flowers
- Create an altar for Obatala with tokens of gold or silver jewelry and images of white elephants, doves, and snails
- Wear white clothing or white jewelry
- Light a white candle in honor of Obatala

Here's a sample personal petition to Obatala:

Obatala, King of the White Cloth, I come to you asking for your blessings and favor. Please assist me along my healing journey by restoring my body to perfect health. Please help me invite more peace into my heart and relationships. Please bring balance and harmony to all I do so I can be an example for others. Thank you. Thank you. Thank you.

Oonagh (Deity, Irish)

Oonagh is a high queen of the fairies of the Tuatha Dé Danaan and the goddess of both love and young animals. She is married to Fionnbhart, the king. The Sidhe (fae) were the first inhabitants of Ireland before retreating underground after the Gaels invaded the land. Fionnbhart's affairs with mortal women were legendary; however, his infidelities did not diminish Oonagh's power. She was portrayed as the most beautiful of the fairies, dressed in sparkly silver robes with long, flowing golden hair that reached the ground.

Oonagh can assist with healing romantic relationships, inner strength, body-image issues, depression, healing animals, cultivating joy, developing an exercise routine, and self-care.

To synchronize with the loving energies of Oonagh, try one or more of the following:

- Light a silver candle in Oonagh's honor
- Dance while listening to lively, fun music that lifts your spirits
- Decorate your home with fresh flowers
- Meditate in a garden of flowers

Here's a sample personal petition to Oonagh:

Dearest Oonagh, Beautiful One, Queen of the Fairies, grant me your favor. Send me the blessing of love and romance. Heal my relationships and any wounds buried deep within my heart. Please assist me with experiencing greater joy in my daily life and embracing my sensual nature. Please help me to sparkle and shine as you do. With a grateful heart, I give you thanks. Thank you. Thank you. Thank you.

Oshun (Deity, Yoruban/West African)

The orisha Oshun is a powerful river goddess associated with love, sensuality, family beauty, and wealth. She presides over everything that flows, such as water, money, love, honey, and a mother's milk.[15] She possesses extraordinary divination skills and is a master magician as well as a prolific healer. She is a patient and compassionate spirit whose mythology credits her for being a messenger to the Supreme Creator and a protector of Yorubaland against invaders. However, she does not work well with Oya, and care should be taken not to honor them together.

Oshun can be envisioned as a bejeweled, beautiful woman with long hair. She is typically dressed in golden-yellow clothing adorned with

---

15. Illes, *Encyclopedia of Spirits,* 801.

pearls, bells, and shells. She carries a gourd filled with honey, representing her connection to sensuality.

Oshun can assist with healing family dynamics, matters of the heart, healing from sexual trauma, fertility issues, body-image issues, cultivating joy, and problems connecting with your intuition. She is known to assist with physical healing, especially when traditional treatments are ineffective. She can bestow abundance, of course, including an abundance of health and wealth.

To bond with the loving energies of Oshun, try one or more of the following:

- Light a yellow or gold candle in Oshun's honor
- Wear bright, colorful clothes—a favorite of Oshun
- Walk or sit by a river and connect with the healing properties of the flowing water
- Give offerings such as chamomile tea, honey, flowers, and jewels
- Meditate with crystals, such as coral, topaz, amber, or malachite

Here's a sample personal petition to Oshun:

Beautiful Oshun of the Sweet Water, please look kindly upon me and stand by my side. Please help heal and strengthen my family relationships. Assist me with releasing any negative body-image issues and increase my ability to love myself as well as others. I respectfully ask for abundance and good fortune to flow seamlessly into my life. With a grateful heart for all your blessings, I give you thanks. Thank you. Thank you. Thank you.

Oya or Aja (Deity, Yoruban/West African)

Oya (also spelled Aja) is an orisha, a goddess of the Yoruba people of southwestern Nigeria. She is known for her healing abilities and willingness to teach healing crafts to others. She is one of the seven main orishas presiding over the woods and all the varieties of plants that grow there.

Her name means "Wild Wind," and like the wind, she is ever-changing and powerful. She is often pictured wearing a skirt of rainbow colors and a beaded veil. In addition, Oya may appear to be holding a lightning bolt due to her association with the weather and powerful storms. Due to the tension between Oya and Oshun, they should not be honored together.

Oya can assist with all types of healing, dramatic transformation of any area in your life, releasing anger, protection, and the process of death and dying.

To bond with the powerful energies of Oya, try one or more of the following activities:

- Develop an affinity for the wind. Sit in a field or on a hill and experience the sensations of the wind against your skin. Listen to the wind rustling through the trees.
- Spend time in the woods walking or hiking
- Create a simple altar with flowers and fruits associated with Oya, such as hibiscus, geraniums, marigolds, papayas, plantains, yams, or strawberries
- Diffuse essential oils such as cinnamon, myrrh, and sandalwood
- Meditate with stones like pietersite, red coral, copper, or amethyst

Here's a sample personal petition to Oya:

Orisha Oya, of the wind and lightning, please hear my request. As you have the power of the storms, please share your dynamic energies of change and profound healing knowledge with me. Please provide me with your protection and strength to overcome any adversity. With your assistance, may I receive healing, hope, and transformation, both for myself and those in need. Thank you. Thank you. Thank you.

Pachamama (Deity, Inca)

Pachamama is the great earth goddess of the Incas. She is the sacred mother that provides nourishment and sustenance to her people. According to her mythology, she gave humanity the gift of agriculture and medicinal herbs. Although Pachamama represents the earth herself, she may appear as a beautiful woman wearing a red dress cloaked with a shawl made from the wool of a llama, an animal sacred to her. She is also described as a dragon living under the mountains that, when angered, shakes the ground in the form of an earthquake.

Pachamama may be called to assist with fertility issues, the ability to absorb nutrients, food allergies, stress, anxiety, protection, releasing anger and toxic emotions, and overall well-being.

To bond with the nurturing energies of Pachamama, try one or more of the following:

- Offerings of cornmeal, beer, or wine poured as a libation directly on the earth
- Donate to environmental causes
- Spend time observing the world around you with a sense of appreciation and awe
- Meditate with crystals such as kambaba stone, serpentine, and turquoise

Here's a sample personal petition to Pachamama:

Pachamama, Earth Mother, I appreciate the beauty of the land on which I live and am grateful for the food that sustains me. As I open myself up to form a deeper connection to the earth and its wonders, I ask that you share your creative energies with me so I can create greater health, abundance, and happiness in my life. Please guide me as to how I can contribute to the healing of this planet and be a guiding light for others. Thank you. Thank you. Thank you.

Padre Pio (Saint)

Originally named Francisco Forgione, Padre Pio was born in Pietrelcina, Italy, on May 25, 1887, to humble farmers who encouraged Francisco's dedication to the church. Unfortunately, illness plagued his childhood and teenage years; he suffered from gastroenteritis, typhoid fever, and poor overall health. Upon reaching the age of fifteen, Francisco entered the religious order of the Capuchin friars and took the name "Pio," honoring Pope Pius I. In 1910, Brother Pio became an ordained priest.

Padre Pio became an international figure for his charity, devotion, preaching style, and his affliction with stigmata, the spontaneous appearance of the wounds suffered by Jesus Christ during the crucifixion. He also performed documented miracles during his lifetime, including reports of levitation, spontaneous healings, and predictions about the future. Padre Pio passed away on September 23, 1968, and was later recognized as a saint by Pope John Paul II. Padre Pio's feast day is September 23.

Saint Padre Pio can be called upon for healing on all levels: physical, mental, emotional, and spiritual. He can also provide assistance with forgiveness, anxiety, depression, increasing your healing abilities, and spiritual development.

To develop a rapport with the healing energies of Saint Padre Pio, try one or more of the following:

- Start a personal forgiveness practice
- Light a white candle in honor of Padre Pio
- Meditate upon the image of Padre Pio to connect with his healing energies

Here's a sample personal petition to Saint Padre Pio:

*Dearest Padre Pio, please turn your kind gaze toward me. I invite
your presence into my life. As you performed miraculous healings
during your lifetime and after you went to your heavenly home,
I humbly ask for your blessings for miraculous healing in my life.*

Please share your gifts of forgiveness and healing with me, not only for my personal benefit but also so that I can be of service to others. Thank you. Thank you. Thank you.

Pele (Deity, Hawaiian)

Pele is the goddess of volcanoes and fire. She has the ability to create as well as destroy. Known for both her fiery temper and her generosity, she is credited for creating islands as she traveled by canoe from her original home island (some say Tahiti) to her current residence on the Big Island of Hawaii. Her myths describe her affinity for music and dancing as well as delicious food and drink. Her passionate love affairs are numerous. She can appear in any form that she wishes but is often depicted as a beautiful woman dressed in red garments with long hair that may be colored black, white, red, or silver. Please note that you should not include both Pele and Poliʻahu, the Hawaiian goddess of snow, in your Divine Support System at the same time since they are not compatible with each other.

Pele can provide assistance with vitality, courage, and passion. She can act as a protective guardian or can aid with healing metabolism problems, digestive issues, healing from sexual trauma, the release of anger and jealousy, personal empowerment, and radical transformation of any area of your life.

To align with the dynamic energies of Pele, try one or more of the following:

- Create an altar for Pele, including images of volcanoes, figurines of sharks and dogs, flowers, and red or orange silk scarves
- Light a red candle in Pele's honor
- Honor your passionate side: dance, listen to music, and eat delicious food with your love interest
- Meditate with stones associated with Pele, such as lava stone, obsidian, and fire agate

Here's a sample personal petition to Pele:

Pele, Goddess of Fire, I call to you. Dear One Who Shapes the Sacred Land, I ask that you share your dynamic energy of healing and transformation with me, shaping my life into one of perfect health and happiness. Light my own divine inner flame, bringing me clarity of mind and purpose. Bless me with vitality and unlimited energy. Heal my physical body. Awaken my dormant passions. Please assist me in transforming my life, enabling me to reach all my wellness goals. Thank you. Thank you. Thank you.

Poli'ahu (Deity, Hawaiian)

Poli'ahu is the goddess of snow and sacred water, living atop Mauna Kea, Hawaii's highest dormant volcano. Poli'ahu is an approachable, friendly goddess with a compassionate heart. She is said to be the most beautiful of all the goddesses, and her romantic liaisons are legendary.

Her myths include her rivalry with her sister, the fire goddess Pele. In one tale, Pele disguises herself and challenges Poli'ahu to a sledding race down the slopes of Mauna Kea. Poli'ahu won two races before Pele called forth fiery lava that melted the snow. Enraged that she had been tricked, Poli'ahu created a powerful snowstorm to extinguish Pele's fire and blanketing Mauna Kea in snow in perpetuity.

Poli'ahu can assist with all types of healing, creating abundance, assisting with fertility issues, healing relationships, sibling rivalry, and clarity of mind.

To connect with the healing energies of Poli'ahu, try one or more of the following:

- Create an altar for Poli'ahu decorated with snowflakes
- Donate to charities involved with clean water
- Light a silver candle in her honor
- In colder weather, partake in outdoor activities such as snowshoeing, sledding, skiing, ice skating, and hiking
- Meditate with crystals, such as larimar and white coral

Here's a sample personal petition to Poliʻahu:

Dearest Poliʻahu, Most Beautiful One of the Whitest Snow, I come to with a pure heart asking for your assistance. May I receive your blessings for an abundance of health. Increase my mental clarity and focus to achieve all my healing goals. Transform any friction and strife in my life and my relationships into perfect harmony. With a grateful heart, I give you thanks. Thank you. Thank you. Thank you.

Psyche (Deity, Greek)

Meaning "soul" and "butterfly" in Greek, Psyche is also a compassionate goddess of love and of the soul. According to her mythology, Psyche was once a charming princess whose beauty inspired the worship of others, such that some said she was even more beautiful than Aphrodite. Enraged by the competition, Aphrodite sent her son Eros to curse Psyche by shooting his arrow of love at her, thereby causing her to fall deeply in love with an unsuitable match. However, Eros became so enamored with the sleeping Psyche that he accidentally scratched himself with his own arrow and instantly became infatuated with her. Psyche's sisters became so jealous of Psyche's beauty that her father sent her away for her own safety. (In some versions, the Oracle at Delphi tells the king that Psyche is doomed to marry a hideous monster and that she should be left chained to a rock. The heartbroken king complies, but unbeknownst to him, Eros was watching.) After rescuing and marrying her, Eros didn't reveal his true identity; he only approached her at night, shrouded in darkness. Psyche returned his passion and was allowed to live with him in his beautiful palace under one condition: that she never look upon him.

Although they were blissfully happy, Psyche eventually used the light of a lamp to gaze upon her lover to see his true identity, awakening him when some oil from the lamp spilled on his shoulder. Her shocked and betrayed husband fled from Psyche in despair. In her search for who she now knew was the god Eros, Psyche was left with no choice but to ask

Aphrodite to find her son's whereabouts. Figuring out what had happened and still irate, Aphrodite sent Psyche off on a grueling, impossible quest into the underworld, where she died. Eros eventually rescued her from this fate and brought her to Mount Olympus, where she was gifted with immortality. She can be pictured as a beautiful young woman with butterfly wings.

Psyche can assist with forgiveness, healing the subconscious mind, understanding your subconscious drives, healing relationships with mothers-in-law and siblings, healing romantic relationships, and healing the soul.

If you'd like to connect with Psyche's loving and supportive energies, try one or more of the following:

- Create an altar to Psyche, including images of butterflies
- Light a pink candle in her honor
- Read myths about Psyche, such as *The Golden Ass* by Lucius Apuleius
- Meditate with crystals associated with Psyche, such as lepidolite, dolomite, or quartz

Design a personal petition to Psyche. Below is an example for reference:

Goddess Psyche, embrace me with your butterfly wings. Beautiful one, I ask for your blessings of healing. Please assist me in healing all of my relationships that are currently strained. Help me heal traumas and past hurts still present in my subconscious mind and deep within my heart. Please help me to forgive all those who have hurt me. Grant me deep healing on the soul level, increasing my connection to the Divine and my life's purpose. I am so grateful for your intervention and support. Thank you. Thank you. Thank you.

Raguel (Archangel)

Archangel Raguel is an amiable angel whose name means "Friend of God." In the apocryphal Book of Enoch, Archangel Raguel is listed as one of the seven archangels and is specifically the angel of Earth. One of Raguel's functions is to oversee the entire community of angels, a role that led to his being referred to as the "angel of justice and fairness." Archangel Raguel may be visualized wearing pale blue robes.

Under Pope Zachary in 745 CE, Archangel Raguel and other angels were removed from the official listing of angels recognized by the church as a response to the growing popularity of angels among the congregation. By Pope Zachary's decree, any angel who was not explicitly mentioned in the scriptures would not be recognized.

You can ask Archangel Raguel for assistance with conflict resolution, personal empowerment, inner peace, healing relationships of any kind, maintaining and strengthening personal boundaries, and achieving balance.

If you'd like to connect with Archangel Raguel's powerful energies, try one or more of the following:

- Help those in need, especially marginalized groups and those considered underdogs
- Light a light blue candle in honor of Archangel Raguel
- Cultivate the qualities of fairness and justice within yourself

Here's a sample personal petition to Archangel Raguel:

Archangel Raguel, Friend of God, please hear my petition and respond swiftly. I humbly ask your assistance in achieving inner peace and harmony, facilitating deep healing on all levels of my being: physically, mentally, emotionally, and spiritually. Please help me resolve conflicts in my relationships, attract friends and allies, and remove stress from my daily life. Please empower me to make wise choices and take actions that lead to health and greater well-being. Thank you. Thank you. Thank you.

Raphael (Archangel)

Archangel Raphael is one of the premier angels of healing in the Judeo-Christian tradition. In fact, the name *Raphael* traces its roots to the

Hebrew *rapha*, which means "doctor" or "healer," rendering his name to mean "God Has Healed." In addition to being affiliated with healing and medicine, Archangel Raphael is associated with the air element, the direction of the east, and the spring season. Archangel Raphael is often depicted wearing golden robes and holding a staff.

In the Kabbalistic tradition, Archangel Raphael is said to be responsible for the healing of both Abraham after he was circumcised and Abraham's son, Jacob, after he was wounded in the thigh during a battle. Archangel Raphael is also credited with guarding the Tree of Life in the Garden of Eden as well as escorting newly departed souls to the afterlife. Additionally, Archangel Raphael is credited in Catholicism with numerous miraculous healings, and September 29 is his feast day (as he is also recognized as a saint).

Archangel Raphael can assist with any healing, including (but not limited to) physical healing, healing from addictions, mental health issues, learning disabilities, ADHD, healing for others, and healing of pets.

To align with the healing energies of Archangel Raphael, try one or more of the following:

- Spend time outside feeling the fresh air on your skin and the breeze on your face
- Engage in activities that utilize your intellect, such as reading and solving puzzles
- Watch a sunrise and appreciate its beauty

Here's a sample personal petition to Archangel Raphael:

Archangel Raphael, please turn your healing gaze upon me. As the angel of springtime and new beginnings, I call upon you as I begin a journey toward greater health and happiness. I need healing and humbly request your assistance. Please restore my health on all layers and all levels: physically, mentally, emotionally, and spiritually. Please fill me with your healing energies and grace so that I will be restored to optimal health. I am grateful for your presence in my life and my heart. Thank you. Thank you. Thank you.

Salamanders (Elemental)

Salamanders are the elementals associated with fire. Characteristics and associations of this element are the spiritual body, faith, regulating body temperature, vitality, personal power, confidence, determination, enthusiasm, and accessing both passion and inspiration. Salamanders are the elemental beings that can assist us with deepening our connection to the fire element and embodying these aspects. The salamanders can be pictured as fiery lizards about a foot in length. Whenever you light a fire or a candle, the salamanders are present. The salamanders are governed by a monarch named Djinn, who can be envisioned as tall as a human dressed in robes of red, orange, and yellow, with flames dancing in his eyes.

Healing with the fire element and the salamanders can assist us with healing the spiritual body, regulating metabolism and internal body temperature, increasing vitality, standing confidently in our personal power, developing our willpower, and connecting with our passions.

If you'd like to attune to the stimulating energies of the salamanders, try one or more of the following:

- Meditate using a candle as your focal point, visualizing the fiery lizard-shaped salamanders in the flickering flame
- Engage in activities that ignite your passions
- Read myths, fairy tales, and folktales about the fire elementals, such as salamanders and other fire spirits of nature, such as genies, firebirds, and dragons
- Meditate with fiery crystals, such as fire agate, carnelian, and orange calcite

Here's a sample personal petition to Djinn, the monarch of the salamanders:

Dearest Djinn, Monarch of the Salamanders, I humbly ask that you hear these words and answer my request. Please help me to connect on an intimate level with the energies of the fire element. Please help to heal my spiritual body and provide me with the faith

*needed to continue my healing journey. Please assist me with ob-
taining greater vitality, living a life filled with passion, and standing confidently in my personal power. Finally, please help me to
shine my light brightly in the world and share my inner light with
others. Thank you. Thank you. Thank you.*

Sandalphon (Archangel)

In the angelic lore of the Old Testament, Archangel Sandalphon is the
prophet Elijah, who rose up and transfigured into a heavenly being. The
name *Sandalphon* could be from Greek: *syn-* or *sym-* meaning "with,"
and *adelphos* meaning "brother" or "co-brother," possibly a reflection of
the close, brotherly relationship between the archangels Sandalphon and
Metatron, another archangel who is said to have once been a human (the
prophet Enoch). Archangel Sandalphon is described as extremely tall
and may be visualized wearing light brown robes and carrying a cornucopia.

Archangel Sandalphon is credited for collecting and delivering prayers
to the creator. In addition, he is the angel assigned to the tenth sphere of
the Tree of Life, Malkuth, representing Earth and the physical realm.

Archangel Sandalphon can be called upon to assist with financial
health and abundance, healing the physical body, manifesting your inner
vision into the material realm, grounding, connecting to the earth, healing from anxiety and stress, and delivering prayers to the creator.

To align with the grounding energies of Archangel Sandalphon, try
one or more of the following:

- Walk barefoot on the grass or sand, feeling a deep connection
  to the earth
- Place a cornucopia, the horn of plenty, in a prominent place in
  your home
- Diffuse juniper berry or sandalwood essential oils

Here's a sample personal petition to Archangel Sandalphon:

Archangel Sandalphon, please hear these words. I ask for your assistance with the profound healing of both my physical body and my finances. I ask that my connection to Mother Earth be strengthened, providing me with the stability, balance, and grounding that I require at this time of my life. Please assist me with manifesting my goals of optimal health and wellness into the material plane. Please deliver these prayers to the Creator with my love and gratitude. Thank you. Thank you. Thank you.

Saule (Deity, Baltic)

Saule is one of the most adored goddesses of the Baltic pantheon. She is both the goddess of the sun and the mother of the universe. In Baltic mythology, she is the mother goddess whose daughters are the planets. She travels across the heavens during the day in her chariot pulled by golden horses. At night, she descends into the ocean to wash her horses before journeying in a golden boat into the underworld. She was once married to the moon, Menulis, but separated from him after he assaulted her daughter. As a result of his deplorable actions, Saule slashed the moon's face and vowed to no longer be seen in his presence. She can be envisioned as an attractive, regal woman cloaked in gold with long golden hair and a golden crown.

The energies of Saule are both powerful and nurturing. Saule may be called to assist with issues involving healing on all levels of your being, vitality, fertility, pregnancy, depression, anxiety, standing in your personal power, and recovery from sexual trauma.

To align with the healing energies of Saule, try one or more of the following:

- Give offerings of apples, roses, and daisies
- Spend time enjoying the sunlight, using the necessary safety precautions
- Visualize golden light completely saturating your body with healing energy

- Meditate with golden or solar crystals such as amber and orange calcite

Here's a sample personal petition to Saule:

O Radiant One, Saule, shine your loving light upon me and fill me with your radiant healing energies. Grant me vitality, health, longevity, and happiness. Please help me to shine my light in the world with confidence and assist me in standing in my personal power. Please hear my requests and grant me your blessings. Thank you. Thank you. Thank you.

Sekhmet (Deity, Egyptian)

Sekhmet, a lioness-headed goddess of ancient Egypt, is widely known for her warrior qualities and healing abilities. *Sekhmet* means "Powerful" or "the Female Power." She is considered a solar deity and is often depicted with the solar disk on top of her head.

In Egyptian mythology, Sekhmet's fiery, hot breath created the desert, and she was responsible for the plagues and illnesses that befell Egypt's people. However, Sekhmet was also known for her healing powers. She was invoked during prayers for the sick and to guard against diseases. Her priests were considered among the best physicians in ancient Egypt.

The energies of Sekhmet are both energizing and healing. Sekhmet may be called to assist with issues involving healing for all levels of your being: physical, mental, emotional, and spiritual. She can also assist with protection, vitality, metabolism issues, reproductive issues, self-confidence, depression, anxiety, willpower, and standing in your personal power.

If you'd like to bond with Sekhmet's powerful energies, try one or more of the following:

- Connect with the energies of the sun by watching a sunrise or sunset
- Meditate on a flickering candle to connect with the fire element associated with Sekhmet

- Create a simple altar with a picture or sculpture of Sekhmet
- Diffuse essential oils such as neroli, white lotus, and sandalwood
- Make an offering to Sekhmet of pomegranates, beer, or incense
- Meditate with crystals such as tiger's eye, yellow jasper, bloodstone, or orange calcite

Here's a sample personal petition to Sekhmet:

Sekhmet, Mighty One, please hear this request and shine your light upon me. I humbly ask for your assistance with deep healing on all layers and levels of my being. I ask that all illness and disease be burned away by your healing fire, resulting in the restoration of my health. Please assist me in brightly shining my light in the world and confidently standing in my personal power. With a grateful heart, I give you thanks. Thank you. Thank you. Thank you.

Serapis Bey (Ascended Master)

Serapis Bey is an Ascended Master who was possibly the Greco-Egyptian god Serapis, who presided over birth and fertility as well as death and the afterlife. He is an original member of the Great White Brotherhood of Light, a group of Ascended Masters with the goal of assisting humankind with their spiritual evolution. His primary responsibility is for the ascension of humankind. Serapis Bey is often portrayed as a man wearing a white turban or headdress.[16]

Serapis Bey can assist with improving physical fitness, weight loss, addictions, spiritual health, inner peace, and strengthening your connection to the Divine.

To connect with the motivating and loving energies of Serapis Bey, try one or more of the following:

- Light a white candle in Serapis Bey's honor
- Begin a fitness and/or nutrition plan

---

16. Illes, *Encyclopedia of Spirits,* 897.

- Cultivate a state of inner peace, whether through meditation or walking in nature

Develop a personal petition to Serapis Bey such as the following:

Beloved Serapis Bey, I call your name to invite you to take an active role in my personal evolution. I ask that you come to me as a guide and coach, providing me insights and motivation to reach my goals of greater health and overall well-being. Please assist me with nurturing my body, mind, and soul. Bring peace into my heart and to all of humanity. Thank you. Thank you. Thank you.

Shekinah (Deity, Mystic Christian)

Shekinah, the Bride of God, is the female aspect of God. Her name is derived from the Hebrew word meaning "dwelling," as she represents the divine presence accessible around and within us. According to esoteric writings, Shekinah and YHVH (the Tetragrammaton, a divine name of God with a masculine aspect) harmoniously dwelled together in the Holy of Holies, the sacred inner chamber of the Jewish temple in Jerusalem. Together, they united the masculine and feminine energies to promote balance in the world and stimulated the creation process. After the Roman army destroyed and looted the holy temple in 70 CE, the balancing and creative energies of the two divine aspects of God found within the temple were severed.

Shekinah dwells within the world and can be called upon for healing and protection. She can be pictured as a dove, a bride wearing white garments, or a woman in mourning for her loss and the persecution of her people. Her nature is compassionate and nurturing, and she can assist with protection and healing on all levels: physical, emotional, mental, and spiritual. She can help heal relationships and with forming meaningful connections with others. Additionally, she can aid in the grieving process and alleviate depression.

If you'd like to form a connection to Shekinah's healing energies, try one or more of the following:

- Engage in acts of creation such as writing, gardening, painting, and pottery
- Spend time meaningfully connecting with others, such as family and friends
- Light a white candle in her honor
- Meditate with crystals, such as purple fluorite, charoite, or amethyst

Here's a sample personal petition to Shekinah:

Dearest Shekinah, Bride of God, I am calling to you in a time of need. Please help heal my wounded heart and alleviate my suffering. Share your nurturing energies with me, revitalizing my physical body, my mind, and my spirit. Envelop me in peace today and all my days. Thank you. Thank you. Thank you.

Shiva (Deity, Hindu)

Shiva, the Lord of Destruction, is one of the three primary deities of the Hindu pantheon, along with Brahma, the creator, and Vishnu, the preserver. His name translates to "Auspicious One," and he is known for eliminating all sorrows and pain. There are many facets to Shiva representing different aspects of his personality: the sadhu (holy person) who has wholly dedicated himself to spiritual practices and renounced everyday life, the adoring husband, the cosmic dancer, and the god of destruction. He is also a master healer willing to assist anyone in need.

Shiva can be envisioned with blue skin, unkempt hair, and wearing animal skins, a necklace made of skulls, and cremation ash on his face. He is portrayed with four arms and four faces. Each face may contain three eyes, with the third eye at the center of each forehead.

Shiva can assist with any type of healing: physical, mental, emotional, and spiritual. He can also help with vitality, fertility issues, destroying negative habits, addictions, compulsive behaviors, depression, cultivating joy, and protection.

If you'd like to bond with the powerful energies of Shiva, try one or more of the following:

- Meditate on a statue or image of Shiva
- Light a blue candle in Shiva's honor
- Drums are associated with Shiva. Join a drumming circle or drum as part of your meditation practice.
- Give offerings, such as flowers, fruit, coconuts, and nuts
- Recite the mantra *Shiva Hum* (pronounced "SHEE-vah hoom"). Mantras are traditionally recited 108 times over forty days, but feel free to modify this practice as needed.

Here's a sample personal petition to Shiva:

Lord Shiva, I ask that you assist me along my journey toward greater health and happiness. As the god of destruction, please eliminate any negative habits, fears, and outdated modes of thinking that are preventing me from reaching my healing goals. Assist me in releasing anger and inviting more peace into my heart and my life. Fill me with joy, passion, and vitality so I can live my best life. With a grateful heart for your presence in my healing journey, I give you thanks. Thank you. Thank you. Thank you.

Sylphs (Elemental)

Sylphs are the elementals associated with air, which is related to the mental body, clarity of thought, balance, harmony, and communication skills, including speaking and writing. Sylphs can assist us with deepening our connection to the air element and embodying these characteristics. The sylphs can be pictured as delicate, etheric beings who may appear human-like or in the form of winged creatures such as birds. The sylphs are governed by a monarch named Paralda, who can be envisioned with long, flowing silver hair and delicate facial features. Paralda wears a gossamer silver robe lined with sky-blue trim.

Healing with the air element and the sylphs can assist with healing the mental body, developing clarity of mind, alleviating anxiety, learning disabilities, ADHD, improving focus and memory, and developing greater communication skills.

If you'd like to attune to the healing energies of the sylphs, try one or more of the following:

- Meditate using your breath as a focal point, inhaling and exhaling for an equal amount of time. For example, inhaling for a count of four, five, or six and then exhaling for the same count of four, five, or six.
- Spend time outdoors on a windy day, feeling the sensation of air on your skin
- Listen to the sounds of nature, such as the chirping of birds or the wind through the trees
- Read myths, fairy tales, and folktales about the air elementals such as sylphs and other air spirits
- Meditate with crystals associated with the air element, such as apatite, celestite, and howlite

Here's a sample personal petition to Paralda:

Dearest Paralda, Monarch of the Sylphs, please hear these words and answer my request. Please help me to connect on an intimate level with the energies of the air element. Please assist me with obtaining greater mental health, providing me with clarity of mind and improved focus. Please help me to develop my communication skills so I clearly and creatively express myself. Please help me to find inner balance and live in harmony. I am so grateful for your assistance. Thank you. Thank you. Thank you.

Tara (Deity, Buddhist, Hindu; Bodhisattva; Ascended Master)

There are two origin stories for the goddess and bodhisattva Tara. The first describes a youthful princess named Yesha Dawa ("Wisdom Moon") in a realm known as Multicolored Light, who attracted the attention of Buddhist monks with her devotion and wisdom. These monks were astonished and urged her to pray to be reborn as male so she could advance further in her next incarnation. Yesha Dawa rebuked them and vowed only to attain enlightenment in female incarnations and to work tirelessly for the enlightenment of all beings, becoming Tara, the Universal Mother.

The second is the story of Avalokitésvara's tears, in which the significant bodhisattva Avalokitésvara (more commonly known as Kwan Yin) pledged to liberate all sentient beings, stating that if he ventured away from this vow, he would shatter into countless fragments. With great effort, he did work on this task but hesitated when he realized how many beings needed liberation. Once he paused his quest, he fractured into a million pieces. Devastated, buddhas and bodhisattvas tediously put the pieces of Avalokitésvara together again, restoring his health. Avalokitésvara began to cry a pool of tears of compassion for humankind. A beautiful lotus emerged from this pool of tears, and Tara, the goddess of compassion, emerged from its center.

Tara takes on numerous forms portrayed by different colors (red, black, blue, yellow, orange, green, and white), each associated with her various personas. In her green and white forms, Tara is a compassionate and benevolent goddess who readily assists with healing. Green Tara can provide swift assistance by bringing more happiness into your life, alleviating suffering, helping with fertility issues and overall health, and reducing fear, stress, and anxiety. She can be pictured as a youthful girl with green skin sitting on a lotus. White Tara is known as the Healing Tara and can assist with any health-related issue, provide longevity, and assist with financial healing, enlightenment, and inner peace. She can be envisioned as a young woman with dark blue hair and seven eyes, three on her face as well as the palms of her hands and the soles of her feet, seated in a meditation posture upon a lotus emerging from a lake.

To align with the loving energies of Tara, try one or more of the following:

- Light a white or green candle in honor of Tara
- Provide food to those in need—people, sheltered animals, or birds
- Meditate upon a statue or image of Tara
- Expand your knowledge of Tara by reading books about her various manifestations
- Chant the Sanskrit mantra to Tara: *om tare tuttare ture swaha* (pronounced "aum tah-reh too-tah-rey too-rey swah-ha"). Mantras are traditionally chanted 108 times for forty days, but this practice can be modified for your purposes.
- Meditate with crystals, such as chrysocolla, turquoise, or white jade (for white Tara) or green jade (for green Tara)

Here's a sample personal petition to Tara, specifically White Tara:

I call upon White Tara, the Healing Tara, Queen of Compassion. Gaze upon me with your seven eyes and observe that I have embarked on a journey of healing and personal growth. Please remove all obstacles along my path. Please assist me with healing on all levels of my being: physical, emotional, mental, and spiritual. Fill me with your compassion and bring peace to my heart, relationships, and home. Thank you. Thank you. Thank you.

Thérèse of Lisieux (Saint)

Saint Thérèse of Lisieux was born in France on January 2, 1873. As the youngest child, she was adored by her older siblings and parents. She was called "little flower," due in part to her delicate nature. At age fifteen, she answered the call to serve God and joined the Carmelite Order of nuns. Although she suffered from tuberculosis, she maintained her faith and dedicated herself to love. In her popular autobiography, *The Story of a Soul*, she describes how significant, demonstrative acts are not necessary to live a holy life; instead, the focus of one's life should be love. Passing away in 1897 at the age of twenty-four, Saint Thérèse of Lisieux was canonized in 1925.

Saint Thérèse of Lisieux can be called upon to assist with the healing process; for protection; to help those struggling with addiction, anxiety, or depression; and for those in spiritual crisis.

To develop a connection to the healing energies of Saint Thérèse of Lisieux, try one or more of the following:

- Practice small, random acts of kindness
- Place red or pink roses in a predominant place in your home
- Meditate with crystals such as rose quartz, pearl, or pink chalcedony
- Explore the concept of love by journaling or reading poetry about love

Here's a sample personal petition to the Saint Thérèse of Lisieux:

Saint Thérèse of Lisieux, Little Flower, I am inspired by your life story and dedication to the simple act of love. It is my heartfelt intention to connect with your energies of love and healing. Please open my heart so that it can be filled with divine love and grace. Please assist me with my own healing process and with the healing of all those in need. Thank you. Thank you. Thank you.

Undines (Elemental)

Undines are the elementals associated with water and the emotional body, the subconscious mind, fluidity, empathy, and intuition. Undines are the elemental beings that can assist us with deepening our connection to the water element and incorporating these characteristics into ourselves. The undines can be pictured as beautiful mermaids or human-like beings with wavy or watery clothing. The undines are governed by a monarch named Nixsa, who can be envisioned as wearing seafoam-green robes and a crown of sea shells.

Healing with the water element and the undines can assist with healing the emotional body, developing a "go with the flow" approach to life, accessing your subconscious mind, developing empathy and intuition, and achieving greater emotional intelligence.

To attune to the healing energies of the undines, try one or more of the following:

- Meditate near a body of water facing west, the direction associated with the water element
- Take a restorative bath with sea salts
- Listen to music that connects with you on an emotional level
- Read myths, fairy tales, and folktales featuring water elementals such as undines, mermaids, or water nymphs
- Meditate with watery-looking crystals such as aquamarine, larimar, ocean jasper, or blue lace agate

Here's a personal petition to Nixsa:

Dearest Nixsa, Monarch of the Undines, please turn your compassionate gaze my way. Please help me to connect on a deep, emotional level with the energies of the water element. Please assist me with obtaining greater emotional health and increasing my emotional intelligence to form more meaningful relationships. Help me develop and trust my intuition so I can confidently follow my inner guidance. It is with an open and loving heart that I give you thanks. Thank you. Thank you. Thank you.

Uriel (Archangel)

Although not specifically named in the Bible, Archangel Uriel (sometimes spelled *Auriel*) is considered one of the most important angels described in legends and myths. The name *Uriel* means "Hero of God" or "Fire of God" in Hebrew. Archangel Uriel is often credited as being the one who informed Noah of the upcoming apocalyptic flood and the archangel who shared the divine gift of alchemy with the world. Archangel Uriel may be envisioned wearing green robes and holding a cornucopia. Archangel Uriel is associated with the element of earth, the direction of north, and winter.

Archangel Uriel was removed from the official listing of angels under Pope Zachary in 745 CE, an action the church took as a response to the (in their opinion, excessive) popularity of angels among the congregation. By Pope Zachary's decree, any angel not explicitly mentioned in the scriptures would not be recognized by the church. However, Archangel Uriel is still honored as Saint Uriel, with a feast day of September 29.

Archangel Uriel can be called upon to assist with healing the physical body, financial health, healing of issues surrounding the home, problems with stress and anxiety, healing the planet, and climate change issues.

To connect with the healing energies of Archangel Uriel, consider the following practices:

- Spend time in nature: walking, hiking, gardening, or meditating outdoors are all activities that can help facilitate a connection with Archangel Uriel
- Learn about the history of alchemy and how it can be used for personal transformation and healing
- Light a green-colored candle in honor of Archangel Uriel
- Donate to charities that benefit the health of the planet

Here's a sample personal petition to Archangel Uriel:

Archangel Uriel, Hero of God, I call to you to ask for your divine assistance. Please envelope me with your grounding energy to heal and strengthen my physical body and my financial health. Please send peace and stability to my home environment, creating a sanctuary for me, free of stress and anxiety. It is also my heartfelt request that the earth receive your blessing of healing so that every

living creature can benefit from existing on this beautiful planet.
I am eternally grateful for your support. Thank you. Thank you.
Thank you.

Venus (Deity, Roman)

Initially, Venus was a goddess of Italy associated with fertile soil, vegetable gardens, good fortune, and divine blessings. Over time, her attributes were syncretized with Aphrodite, the Greek goddess of love, whereafter Venus became the Roman goddess of love, beauty, and sensuality. The philosopher and writer Lucretius wrote about Venus in his treatise, *On the Nature of Things*, in 50 BCE. In it, he characterizes Venus as the goddess of nature.

Our planet Venus is named after this powerful Roman goddess and was classically referred to as the "morning star" if she appears in the early morning hours and the "evening star" if she appears in the early evening hours.

The goddess Venus can assist with starting or maintaining self-care practices, healing emotional wounds, healing relationship issues, connecting with your sensual nature, and alleviating fertility problems.

To connect with the loving energies of Venus, try one or more of the following:

- Create a kitchen garden
- Take a restorative bath with flowers and herbs
- Place rose quartz in a prominent area of your home
- Read *On the Nature of Things* (in Latin, *De rerum natura*) by Lucretius, available online
- Meditate with stones, such as chrysocolla, malachite, or copper

Here's a sample personal petition to Venus:

Goddess Venus of the Morning and Evening Star, shine your healing light upon me. Joyful One, Abundant One, I call you asking for your blessing and favor. With a loving heart, I ask that you assist me with all my healing endeavors and self-care practices. Please bring more love and joy into my life. Thank you. Thank you. Thank you.

Vishnu (Deity, Hindu)

Vishnu, the Preserver, is one of the three primary deities of the Hindu pantheon, along with Brahma, the creator, and Shiva, the destroyer. Vishnu is responsible for maintaining world order and balance in the universe. When order and harmony are threatened, Vishnu comes to Earth as himself or one of his avatars to preserve justice. Some of Vishnu's most famous avatars are Rama, Krishna, and Buddha.

Vishnu can be envisioned as an elegant young man with blue skin and four arms. He may be pictured holding an object in each hand: a conch shell, a war discus, a club, and a lotus flower. He rides upon the fearless Garuda, the king of birds, a gigantic mythical bird with a hornbill's head and wings sprouting from a human body. Vishnu is often represented as sleeping in the coils of an enormous serpent drifting in the ocean of the cosmos.

Vishnu can assist with any type of healing: physical, mental, emotional, and spiritual. He can also help you achieve balance and harmony, reduce stress and anxiety, alleviate depression and insomnia, and heal body-image issues.

To bond with the powerful energies of Vishnu, try one or more of the following practices:

- Meditate on a statue or image of Vishnu
- Light a blue or yellow candle in Vishnu's honor
- Diffuse blue lotus essential oil
- Recite the mantra *Om Namo Bhagavate Vasudevaya* (pronounced "aum nah-mah bah-gah-vah-teh vah-soo-deh-vah-yah"). Mantras are traditionally recited 108 times over forty days, but feel free to modify this practice as needed.

Here's a sample personal petition to Vishnu:

Lord Vishnu, Preserver of the Universe, I come to you with an open heart, requesting your assistance. Please help me to create harmony in my relationships, my home, and in my work environment. Please help me release the stress and anxiety that have been a part of my daily life. Please act as my guide and teacher, providing me with the tools and resources to achieve my goals of greater health and happiness. With a grateful heart for your presence in my life, I give you thanks. Thank you. Thank you. Thank you.

Yaoji (Deity, Chinese)

Yaoji is a Chinese goddess known for her knowledge of healing herbs and controlling the weather. There are several legends regarding her origins. One of Yaoji's myths describes her as the youngest fairy daughter of the Queen Mother of the West who studied divine magic. However, Yaoji was unsatisfied with her sheltered life in the heavens, so she traveled to Earth with her fairy attendants. She is associated with the Wushan Mountains, where she is said to have changed into the Goddess Mountain. Her fairy attendants and dragons are said to have been transformed into the other mountain peaks of the Wushan range.

Yaoji is a shape-shifter known to take various forms, including a ghost and a beautiful young woman. She may also be pictured riding upon a tiger. In addition, Yaoji often communicates to her devotees in dreams.

Yaoji can assist with learning the healing properties of plants, development of healing skills, overall health, connecting with your sexuality, and general protection.

To align with the loving energies of Yaoji, try one or more of the following:

- Create an altar to Yaoji with images or figures of fairies, dragons, phoenixes, and cranes
- Study the healing properties of herbs
- Read poems and stories connected to the myths of Yaoji
- Meditate with stones of turquoise, jasper, or jade

Here's a sample personal petition to Yaoji:

Dearest Yaoji, Blossoming Lady of the Clouds, turn your loving eyes upon me. I wish to form a deep connection with you and your fairy entourage for the purpose of deep healing and ancient knowledge. Please share your knowledge of healing with me and act as my guide, teaching me the healing power of plants and other healing modalities. Please act as my guardian, providing me with protection. Please grant me your blessings of health and happiness today and all of my days. With a grateful heart, I give you thanks. Thank you. Thank you. Thank you.

Yemaya (Deity, Yoruban/West African)

Yemaya, Queen of the Sea, is the most prominent of the orishas. This beloved goddess is associated with motherhood, women's issues, and the sea. Yemaya may be depicted as a beautiful, sensual woman wearing seven skirts adorned with pearls, corals, little bells, and crystals.[17] Alternatively, Yemaya may appear in the form of a mermaid. Her name means "the Mother Whose Children Are Fish," a reference to her role as mother of many orishas as well as her capacity to act as a mother to those connected with her.

In the mythology, Yemaya found her sister, Oshun, impoverished after she was cast out from the lands she once ruled as queen. Oshun was washing the only piece of clothing she now owned at the river's edge, a once-white dress now yellowed. Yemaya's compassion for her sister prompted her to change her yellow dress into a golden one, proclaiming that all gold would now belong to Oshun and that her sister's fortune would be restored. Additionally, Yemaya cut off her own hair to create a wig for Oshun, who had lost hers due to the stress of her impoverished state. Yemaya's assistance depicts her kind-hearted nature and willingness to help those in their time of need.

---

17. Illes, *Encyclopedia of Spirits,* 1021.

Yemaya is a compassionate, nurturing goddess. She can assist with fertility issues, pregnancy, overall health, relationship issues, chronic fatigue, self-esteem, depression, anxiety, and creating a healthy home environment.

To bond with the nurturing energies of Yemaya, try one or more of the following:

- Spend time near a body of water
- Create a simple altar with tokens for Yemaya, such as seashells, small bells, crystals, and pearls
- Take a restorative bath with sea salts
- Give offerings of food such as pomegranates, watermelon, plantain chips, or molasses
- Donate to a charity focused on marine life or ocean conservation
- Meditate with crystals such as coral, pearl, larimar, or turquoise

Here is a sample personal petition to Yemaya:

Yemaya, Queen of the Sea, please hear my words and turn your compassionate gaze upon me. I ask that your cleansing waters pour over me, gently dissolving and diluting anything holding me back from attaining greater health and wellness. Please provide me with protection, guidance, strength, and love as I continue to walk my path of healing and personal growth. With a grateful heart, I give you thanks. Thank you. Thank you. Thank you.

Yogananda (Ascended Master)

Born on January 5, 1893, to a loving and devoted Hindu family in northeastern India near the Himalayan mountains, Paramahansa Yogananda immersed himself in the study of yoga and meditation. In 1920, Yogananda's guru, Babaji, instructed Yogananda to leave India and travel to the United States to spread the teachings and practices of yoga and meditation. Once in the United States, Yogananda founded the Self-Realization

Fellowship and attracted thousands of followers with his message of love, unity, and healing. Yogananda passed away in 1952 in Los Angeles, California.

Although not a deity or saint, Yogananda is an Ascended Master, an enlightened spiritual being who can be called upon for any type of healing, achieving a state of inner peace, and connecting with the energies of divine love.

To connect with the supportive and loving energies of Yogananda, try one or more of the following:

- Practice a mind-body-spirit form of physical exercise such as yoga, tai chi, and qigong
- Spend time in silent meditation
- Practice random acts of kindness
- Read *Autobiography of a Yogi* by Paramahansa Yogananda
- Meditate upon the image of Yogananda

Here's a sample personal petition to Yogananda:

Yogananda, I am inspired by your life story and wish to form a connection with you. Please hear this petition made with a loving heart. I ask for your blessings for physical, mental, emotional, and spiritual healing. Under your guidance and with your assistance, may peace and love live forever in my heart and in the world. Thank you. Thank you. Thank you.

Zadkiel (Archangel)

Archangel Zadkiel is an angel of compassion, benevolence, memory, prosperity, and good fortune. In Hebrew, the name *Zadkiel* means "Righteousness of God." Archangel Zadkiel may be visualized wearing blue robes and holding a scepter or a dagger.

It was Archangel Zadkiel who stopped Abraham from sacrificing his beloved son, Isaac, on Mount Moriah. Zadkiel is also the angel assigned to the fourth sphere of the Tree of Life, Chesed, and the planet Jupiter, which is associated with expansion and good fortune.

You can request Zadkiel to assist you with forgiveness, memory issues, releasing negative attachments, cultivating joy, relief from depression, financial health, removing limiting beliefs, and receiving abundance.

To align with the benevolent energies of Archangel Zadkiel, try one or more of the following:

- Burn bayberry or cedar incense
- Engage in activities that bring joy to your heart
- Light a blue candle in Archangel Zadkiel's honor

Here's a sample personal petition to Archangel Zadkiel:

Archangel Zadkiel, Righteousness of God, please turn your compassionate gaze upon me. I ask for your help with releasing negative thought forms, self-criticism, judgment, past hurts, and anything holding me back from achieving a healthy body and mind. May I receive your blessings of good fortune, especially related to abundance restoring my financial health. With your divine assistance, I will approach each day with joy in my heart. Thank you. Thank you. Thank you.

Chapter 11

Crystal Spirit Allies

Here, you'll find different crystals that can be used for overall healing, each with its own characteristics. This listing is just a sample of the extensive world of crystals available to incorporate into your Divine Support System. How do you pick the right crystal for you? You could select a crystal based on its healing attributes or choose one after finding it using bibliomancy—close your eyes and allow your finger to drift up and down the page until you randomly select one. If there's a metaphysical store near you, another option is to explore their crystal selection and choose whatever crystal "feels" right for you.

Amazonite: Stress reduction, healing communication issues, anxiety, self-confidence

Amber: Protection, abundance, courage

Amethyst: Spiritual healing, inner peace, overall health, accessing psychic abilities

Aquamarine: Overall healing, stress reduction, anxiety, healing communication issues, courage, inner peace, intuition

Aventurine: Financial healing, personal growth

Azurite malachite: Releasing fear, emotional healing, assists with releasing habits and addictive behaviors

Blue chalcedony: Emotional healing, healing communication issues, inner peace

Blue lace agate: Inner peace, releases stress and anxiety, releases fear, emotional balance, healing your home environment, addictions

Carnelian: Protection, intuition, courage, inner peace, forgiveness

Chrysocolla: Issues with self-expression, problems with memory, anxiety, emotional healing, financial healing

Citrine: Self-confidence, willpower, standing in your personal power, digestive issues

Copper: Healing romantic relationships, financial health

Desert rose selenite: Fertility, development of psychic senses, healing of the mental body, ADHD, learning disabilities, protection

Emerald: Healing romantic relationships, protection

Fire agate: Protection, standing in your personal power, vitality, metabolism issues, passion, digestive issues

Green jasper: Financial healing, abundance, grounding, anxiety, depression, healing romantic relationships, self-love

Jade: Inner peace, abundance, protection, connection to dreams

Jet: Protection, healing grief, psychic sense development, releasing fear

Kambaba stone: Grounding, protection, abundance, ancestral healing

Kunzite: Forgiveness, healing romantic relationships, self-love, stress, anxiety, healing home environment, cultivating joy

Lapis lazuli: Intuition development, healing communication issues, courage, protection, visualization, self-confidence (especially in women), ADHD, pregnancy, healing from sexual abuse, mental health

Larimar: Emotional healing, releasing anger, self-confidence, inner peace, anxiety, depression, healing communication issues

Lepidolite: Healing romantic relationships, sleep issues, protection, inner peace, anxiety, stress reduction, depression, ADHD

Malachite: Healing romantic relationships, self-love, success, fertility, standing in your personal power, protection, digestive issues, financial healing

Moonstone: Sleep issues, emotional healing, development of psychic senses

Moss agate: Financial healing, grounding, fertility issues

Obsidian: Protection, intuition, grounding

Ocean jasper: Relationship healing, flexibility of mind, inner peace, anxiety, depression

Orange calcite: Emotional healing, sexual healing, intimacy issues, motivation

Pearl: Relationship healing, self-acceptance, emotional healing, body-image issues, prosperity, financial healing, happiness

Peridot: Financial healing, protection, success, intuition development

Pink chalcedony: Healing of romantic relationships, self-love, healing body-image issues, inner peace

Red coral: Overall healing, vitality, protection

Red jasper: Strength, vitality, courage, grounding, protection, healing of romantic relationships, self-confidence, standing in your personal power

Rose quartz: Forgiveness, healing romantic relationships, self-love, self-acceptance, body-image issues, emotional healing

Selenite: Intuition development, past-life healing, connection to the Divine

Serpentine: Protection, issues with memory, past-life healing, inner peace, abundance

Smoky quartz: Protection, grounding, anxiety, depression

Tiger's eye: Protection, courage, strength, willpower, self-confidence, grounding, intuition development

Turquoise: Healing of friendships, self-love, body-image issues, financial healing, inner peace, connection to the Divine, joy, happiness

White coral: Protection, forgiveness, intuition, strengthening psychic senses

Chapter 12

Plant Spirit Allies

In addition to growing your own plant allies, consider tapping into their healing powers through essential oils, teas, and flower essences. Essential oils are concentrated plant extracts that affect us primarily through our sense of smell and can be diffused through a room or applied topically to the skin. If applying to the skin, use a carrier oil, such as jojoba, to reduce irritation. When brewed as teas, boiling water extracts the healing properties of (edible) herbs, leaves, or flowers. Flower essences are remedies made from the petals of flowers that retain their healing vibrational energy, but it's important to note that flower essences are often made with brandy or vodka. If alcohol isn't an option for you, find a flower essence made with glycerin, use it as a room spray, or apply it topically instead of ingesting it. This chapter represents only a sample of popular plant allies you may incorporate into your Divine Support System.

Essential Oils

The list in this section is partial, representing essential oils that can be used for healing purposes. Texts vary on the healing properties of each essential oil, so experiment and see which oils (or blends of oils) best assist you along your healing journey.

Basil: Promotes happiness, financial healing, abundance, and
inner peace; reduces anxiety; assists with insomnia

Bergamot: Promotes inner peace, reduces anxiety, assists with insomnia and depression

Black pepper: Protection, self-confidence, and vitality

Blue or white lotus: Helps with overall healing, connection to the Divine, and inner peace

Chamomile: Promotes inner peace, assists with insomnia, reduces stress and anxiety

Cypress: Promotes grounding, helps with processing grief, and heals trauma

Eucalyptus: Helps with all types of healing, increases vitality, and reduces fatigue

Frankincense: Helps with strengthening the connection to the Divine, promotes healing of the mental body, increases self-confidence, and helps with emotional healing

Geranium: Assists with overall healing, healing romantic relationships, promotes joy, assists with body-image issues, self-love, and assists with depression

Ginger: Assists with financial health; fosters courage, self-confidence, and personal empowerment

Grapefruit: Alleviates depression; increases vitality, strength, and energy levels; aids in addiction recovery

Jasmine: Assists with healing romantic relationships, strengthening the connection to the Divine, and promotes self-love and forgiveness

Juniper: Helps with overall healing and protection, reduces stress and anxiety, and aids in addiction recovery

Lavender: Promotes inner peace, assists with insomnia, assists
with stress and anxiety relief, and aids in addiction recovery

Lemon: Increases vitality and mental clarity, promotes
optimism, helps with depression, alleviates fatigue of both
body and mind

Lemongrass: Strengthens intuition and the psychic senses,
promotes joy, releases stress and anxiety

Lime: Assists with protection as well as depression and grief,
supports mental clarity, reduces mental fatigue, reduces
anxiety

Myrrh: Enables a connection to the Divine and helps with the
healing of the physical, emotional, mental, and spiritual
body

Neroli: Promotes joy; healing of trauma, including childhood
trauma; emotional healing; assists with grief and depression;
releases fear; helps curb compulsive behaviors

Orange: Supports emotional healing, increases joy and
optimism, assists with depression, helps curb compulsive
behaviors

Palmarosa: Assists with romantic healing, encourages self-love
and self-acceptance, helps with body-image issues

Patchouli: Assists with financial healing, assists with sexual
problems, reduces stress and anxiety, reduces fatigue

Peppermint: Increases vitality, assists with fatigue and
depression, increases strength, promotes mental clarity

Pine: Promotes financial healing, provides protection, helps
with forgiveness—especially self-forgiveness

Rose: Promotes healing relationships of all kinds, strengthens the connection to the Divine, helps with self-love and forgiveness, heals body-image issues

Rosemary: Helps with healing romantic relationships, increases vitality, reduces fatigue, alleviates depression, aids in addiction recovery

Sandalwood: Promotes spiritual connection, encourages mental clarity, reduces stress and anxiety

Tuberose: Reduces stress and anxiety; promotes inner peace, self-love, and self-acceptance

Vetiver: Assists with financial healing, alleviates depression, reduces anxiety, promotes healing of the mental body

Yarrow: Promotes strength and courage, increases self-confidence, provides protection, increases intuition

Ylang-ylang: Promotes inner peace and joy, encourages self-love, assists with healing the emotional body and romantic relationships

Teas

The healing properties of teas have been used across cultures since ancient times. Below is a small sampling of the various healing properties of teas. Teas can be blended based on your unique healing goals. Experiment to see which teas best support your journey toward greater health and happiness. An excellent resource is *Healing Herbal Teas: Learn to Blend 101 Specially Formulated Teas for Stress Management, Common Ailments, Seasonal Health, and Immune Support* by Sarah Farr (Storey Publishing, 2016), which contains recipes for assorted tea blends for stress management, common ailments, and immune support. Before consuming teas, check for any issues due to medications you are taking or physical conditions you might have.

Catnip: Reduces stress and anxiety, assists with insomnia, alleviates headaches

Chamomile: Promotes inner peace, assists with insomnia, reduces stress and anxiety, releases anger

Elderflower: Provides a wealth of physical health benefits and immune support

Hibiscus: Provides a wealth of physical health benefits and antioxidants; promotes joy, passion, and love

Lemon balm leaf: Assists with depression and anxiety, supports healing of the mental body

Mint: Aids digestion, supports emotional and mental healing, promotes optimism

Rose petals: Healing from trauma; assists with forgiveness, self-love, healing of relationships

Skullcap: Supports healing the mental body, helps with addictions and compulsive behaviors

St. John's wort: Aids with depression, anxiety, and insomnia

Tulsi: Assists with memory issues, mental clarity, stress management, immune support, and digestive health

Flower Essences

The development of flower essences is credited to Edward Bach, an English homeopathic physician who developed these healing remedies in the 1930s. The traditional Bach Flower Essences are among the growing number of flower essences available today. A beneficial resource for more information about the healing powers of flower essences is *Flower Essence Repertory: A Comprehensive Guide to the Flower Essences researched by Dr. Edward Bach and the Flower Essence Society* by Patricia Kaminski and Richard Katz (Flower Essences Services, 2004). The listing here is only a small sample of the flower essences available that can assist you in achieving your healing goals.

Acacia: Facilitates emotional healing

Arnica: Assists with recovery from drug or alcohol abuse, addictions

Borage: Promotes courage and confidence

Buttercup: Helps heal issues with self-image and self-esteem

Evening Primrose: Assists with healing from physical, sexual, or emotional abuse

Honeysuckle: Helps with grief, releasing the past

Hornbeam: Alleviates mental exhaustion

Joshua Tree Flower: Supports recovery from ancestral or family-related trauma

Mustard: Alleviates depression, promotes joy and happiness

Olive: Relieves physical exhaustion, promotes vitality

Star of Bethlehem: Supports healing from trauma, assists with grief

White Chestnut: Helps with insomnia, releases stress and anxiety

Conclusion

You Are in Control

There are times when we feel powerless, especially when it comes to health concerns. We can feel overwhelming helplessness and may feel stuck and unable to move forward. However, it is possible to influence our healing path's direction and relationship with our Divine Support System. Although you may face challenges and obstacles, be confident that you are taking the appropriate steps to achieve your healing goals. You can create the conditions necessary for dramatic healing on all levels of being: physical, emotional, mental, and spiritual—embrace your personal power, take charge of your healing process, and collaborate with your Divine Support System.

Power of Choice

As human beings, we are gifted with free will. The more we are self-aware and honestly know ourselves, the more we can understand our motivations and realize our choices define our lives. A key component of standing in your personal power is making choices based on trusting your authentic self and taking the appropriate actions. Throughout your healing journey, you can pick the options that align with your path toward greater health and happiness. Our power of choice relates to our Divine Support System in multiple ways:

- Members of our Divine Support System who will support our healing goals

- The communication methods that reflect our personal preferences
- How we can deepen our relationships with our spirit helpers that resonate with us
- Whether or not to follow guidance and intuitive messages received from our Divine Support System

When we make conscious choices related to our healing path, we actively engage in our lives and take responsibility for our health and happiness. The option to collaborate with your Divine Support System is yours alone; however, these loving and supportive spirit allies are always available if you ask for their assistance.

Precautions: Dos and Don'ts

There are some things you should be aware of as you connect with the unseen realms and your Divine Support System. These pitfalls can be avoided with awareness and self-reflection. Read on for Dos and Don'ts when working with your Divine Support System.

Do

- Practice discernment. Your discretion is both your freedom of choice and your ability to refrain from revealing confidential or private information. Consciously engage with your power of choice at every step of your healing journey and when working with your Divine Support System. Moreover, it's best to use discretion regarding with whom you share information about your Divine Support System. Some people may criticize or joke about your interest in the unseen realms or even try to sabotage your healing efforts. Share your healing journey only with select friends and family members to preserve the sacred nature of your relationships with your Divine Support System.
- Practice moderation. When we are excited about a new practice, idea, or topic, we might spend excessive time dedicated to that

pursuit. Practice moderation when collaborating with your Divine Support System. Develop a realistic schedule that allows time for your everyday activities and relationships. The balance between our spiritual and daily lives is critical for long-term success.

- Explore your shadow side. During your healing sessions, you may be exposed to your shadow side, the parts we all have that we keep hidden due to their association with "negative" and often very old emotions and impulses, such as greed, jealousy, impulsivity, possessiveness, selfishness, and gluttony. If you become aware of your shadow during your healing sessions, consider it an invitation to lean into the experience and explore that quality without judgment so that you can heal and integrate that part of yourself. However, you don't have to examine challenging emotions if you aren't emotionally ready. Use your discretion and make the choice that's best for you now.

- Practice self-care. It's essential that you care for yourself and carve out time to do things that support your overall well-being and improve your physical, emotional, and mental health. Practicing self-care isn't an act of selfishness characterized by prioritizing your needs at the expense of others. Self-care is an act of love in which you are demonstrating the belief that you are worthy of your own care and affection. Self-care also provides us with the internal resources to develop stronger relationships—both in our daily lives and in our Divine Support System.

- Practice respect. If a specific religion or culture interests you, learn and explore more about it under the tutelage of those individuals who actively practice that faith and/or culture. Only conduct work with deities that are universal to all until you are fully immersed in that culture/religion.

Don't

- Expect instant gratification. It's natural to want to experience results immediately. You may encounter some instant benefits upon working with your Divine Support System, but this approach to greater health and wellness typically occurs over time. Be patient—smaller changes and shifts progressively lead to dramatic healing and wellness. By releasing expectations of *when* our healing will happen, we allow our unique process to unfold in the manner that is optimal for us.

- Use alcohol or recreational drugs before communing with your Divine Support System. Alcohol and drugs impair our perceptions and dull our senses. These substances can also leave us susceptible to negative influences. Refrain from any intoxicating substances for at least a day before engaging with your Divine Support System.

- Judge yourself. When working toward greater health and well-being, we often set high expectations for ourselves. We should strive to achieve these high expectations, but if/when we fall short, practice self-compassion—not judgment or negative self-talk. Additionally, we might expect our psychic senses or visualization skills to develop immediately and judge ourselves harshly if they don't emerge rapidly. Be patient with yourself and know that these abilities will unfold and evolve over time.

- Be afraid to ask for help. An essential part of knowing yourself is understanding when you need additional assistance. While working with your Divine Support System, you may need to schedule appointments with medical doctors, mental health professionals, energy workers, or alternative medicine practitioners. Your Divine Support System is not a substitute for professional medical care but can supplement your healthcare practices.

• Give up. A critical component of your personal journey is persisting along your healing path despite the challenges you may face. Keep focused on your goals of greater health and happiness. Your tenacity to follow your schedule of healing sessions with your Divine Support System will produce benefits over time. Don't give up on your dreams of a healthier, happier future.

The Journey Continues

You are beginning an exciting and fulfilling adventure—a quest for greater health and happiness. You are the hero of this story, and the members of your Divine Support System are your supportive companions assisting you with achieving your goals. Your journey may contain obstacles, but with dedication, you will have a rewarding voyage toward wellness.

Take a moment to reflect upon your original goals, wishes, and dreams recorded in your healing journal. Do they still resonate with you? If needed, revise your listing to align with your current objectives and aspirations. Next, consider your Divine Support System intention statement. Read it aloud and explore your emotional response to it. Does it adequately express your purpose for collaborating with your Divine Support System? If not, adjust your intention statement to reflect your updated goals. Your listing of dreams and wishes and your Divine Support System intention statement should be reviewed periodically and expanded, modified, and changed to evolve as you do.

Trust your journey. Your Divine Support System members are ready to support and encourage you along your healing path. The possibilities for greater health and happiness are limitless.

Recommended Reading List

Spirit Guides

How to Meet and Work with Spirit Guides by Ted Andrews is a helpful text to connect and develop relationships with your spirit guides.

Angels

A Dictionary of Angels by Gustav Davidson is a comprehensive guide on a wide variety of angels and angelic lore.

Ancestors

Honoring Your Ancestors: A Guide to Ancestral Veneration by Mallorie Vaudoise gives hands-on techniques and guidance on establishing meaningful connections to the realms of your ancestors.

Animal Spirit Helpers

Animal Spirit Guides: An Easy-to-Use Handbook for Identifying and Understanding Your Power Animals and Animal Spirit Helpers by Stephen D. Farmer is a comprehensive text providing detailed information regarding the types of animal spirit guides and how they can assist you on your life path.

Crystals

The Book of Stones: Who They Are and What They Teach by Robert Simmons and Naisha Ahsian is a comprehensive text providing practical information regarding the background and metaphysical properties of crystals.

Intention Setting

The Power of Intention: Learning to Co-Create Your World Your Way by Dr. Wayne W. Dyer is a useful guide in utilizing the power of intention to help you achieve your goals.

Astrology

Astrology for Yourself: A Workbook for Personal Transformation by Douglas Bloch and Demetra George is an excellent resource for understanding the basics of astrology as well as a deep understanding of your own birth chart.

Essential Oils

The Essential Guide to Aromatherapy and Vibrational Healing by Margaret Ann Lembo is an illuminating text regarding essential oils' healing and energetic properties.

Bibliography

Andrews, Ted. *Enchantment of the Faerie Realms.* Woodbury, MN: Llewellyn Publications, 2012.

———. *How to Meet and Work with Spirit Guides.* Woodbury, MN: Llewellyn Publications, 2011.

Apuleius. *The Golden Ass.* Translated by E. J. Kenney. New York: Oxford University Press, 2004.

Armády, Naha. *Everyday Crystal Rituals: Healing Practices for Love, Wealth, Career, and Home.* Emeryville, CA: Althea Press, 2018.

Ashley-Farrand, Thomas. *Chakra Mantras: Liberate Your Spiritual Genius through Chanting.* San Francisco: Red Wheel/Weiser, 2006.

———. *Healing Mantras: Using Sound Affirmations for Personal Power, Creativity, and Healing.* New York: Random House, 1999.

———. *Shakti Mantras: Tapping Into the Great Goddess Energy Within.* New York: Random House, 2003.

Auset, Brandi. *The Goddess Guide: Exploring the Attributes and Correspondences of the Divine Feminine.* Woodbury, MN: Llewellyn Publications, 2020.

Bloch, Douglas, and Demetra George. *Astrology For Yourself: A Workbook for Personal Transformation.* Berwick, ME: Ibis Press, 2006.

Bottéro, Jean. *Mesopotamia: Writing, Reasoning, and the Gods.* Translated by Zainab Bahrani and Marc Van De Mieroop. Chicago: University of Chicago Press, 1992.

Brown, Coleston, and Gareth Knight. *The Mystery of the Seven Directions*. Vancouver, BC: Magh Mell, 2009.

Bunson, Matthew. *Angels A to Z: Who's Who of the Heavenly Host*. New York: Three Rivers Press, 1996.

Crawford, Jackson, ed. *The Poetic Edda: Stories of the Norse Gods and Heroes*. Indianapolis: Hackett Publishing, 2015.

Covington, Candice. *Essential Oils in Spiritual Practice: Working with the Chakras, Divine Archetypes, and the Five Great Elements*. Rochester, VT: Healing Arts Press, 2017.

Cunningham, Scott. *The Complete Book of Incense, Oils, and Brews*. Woodbury, MN: Llewellyn Publications, 2012.

Davidson, Gustav. *A Dictionary of Angels: Including the Fallen Angels*. New York: Simon and Schuster, 1967.

D'Este, Sorita. *Circle for Hekate–Volume I: History & Mythology*. London: Avalonia Books, 2017.

Dorsey, Lilith. *Orishas, Goddesses, and Voodoo Queens: The Divine Feminine in the African Religious Traditions*. Newburyport, MA: Red Wheel/Weiser, 2020.

Dunn, Patrick. *The Orphic Hymns: A New Translation for the Occult Practitioner*. Woodbury, MN: Llewellyn Publications, 2018.

Echols, Damien. *Angels and Archangels: A Magician's Guide*. Boulder, CO: Sounds True, 2020.

Emmons, Robert, and Michael McCullough, eds. *The Psychology of Gratitude*. New York: Oxford University Press, 2004.

Farmer, Steven D. *Animal Spirit Guides: An Easy-to-Use Handbook for Identifying and Understanding Your Power Animals and Animal Spirit Helpers*. Carlsbad, CA: Hay House, 2006.

Farr, Sarah. *Healing Herbal Teas: Learn to Blend 101 Specially Formulated Teas for Stress Management, Common Ailments, Seasonal Health, and Immune Support*. North Adams, MA: Storey Publishing, 2016.

Gonzales-Wippler, Migene. *Powers of the Orishas: Santeria and Worship of Saints.* Old Bethpage, NY: Original Publications, 1992.

Gray, Kyle. *Divine Masters, Ancient Wisdom: Activations to Connect with Universal Spirit Guides.* Carlsbad, CA: Hay House, 2021.

Gregg, Susan. *Angels, Spirit Guides & Goddesses: A Guide to Working with 100 Divine Beings in Your Daily Life.* Beverly, MA: Quarto Publishing Group, 2009.

Guttman, Arielle. *Venus Star Rising: A New Cosmology for the Twenty-First Century.* Santa Fe: Sophia Venus Publications, 2019.

Hall, Manly P. *Paracelsus, the Four Elements and Their Spirits.* New Haven, CT: Lamp of Trismegistus, 2021.

Humington, Andrew. *The Neuroscience of Gratitude: Why Self Help Has It All Wrong.* Self-published, 2023.

Iles, Judika. *The Encyclopedia of Mystics, Saints & Sages: A Guide to Asking for Protection, Wealth, Happiness, and Everything Else!* New York: HarperCollins, 2011.

———. *The Encyclopedia of Spirits: The Ultimate Guide to the Magic of Fairies, Genies, Demons, Ghosts, Gods & Goddesses.* New York: HarperCollins, 2009.

Judith, Anodea. *Eastern Body, Western Mind: Psychology and the Chakra System as a Path to the Self.* Revised. New York: Crown Publishing Group, 2004.

Kaminski, Patricia, and Richard Katz. *Flower Essence Repertory: A Comprehensive Guide to the Flower Essences researched by Dr. Edward Bach and the Flower Essence Society.* Nevada City, CA: Earth-Spirit, 1994.

Kavanagh, Ambi. *Chakras and Self-Care: Activate the Healing Power of Chakras with Everyday Rituals.* New York: Penguin Random House, 2020.

Kempton, Sally. *Awakening Shakti: The Transformative Power of the Goddess of Yoga.* Boulder, CO: Sounds True, 2013.

Lass, Martin. *Chiron: Healing Body and Soul*. St. Paul, MN: Llewellyn Publications, 2005.

Lehman, J. Lee. *The Ultimate Asteroid Book*. West Chester, PA: Schiffer Publishing, 1988.

Lembo, Margaret Ann. *The Essential Guide to Aromatherapy and Vibrational Healing*. Woodbury, MN: Llewellyn Publications, 2018.

Ovid. *Metamorphoses*. Translated by A. D. Melville. New York: Oxford University Press, 1986.

Monaghan, Patricia. *Encyclopedia of Goddesses and Heroines*. Novato, CA: New World Library, 2010.

Morford, Mark, Robert J. Lenardon, Michael Sham. *Classical Mythology*. New York: Oxford University Press, 2001.

Moss, Robert. *The Secret History of Dreaming*. Novato, CA: New World Library, 2009.

Olson, Dale W. *The Pendulum Instruction Chart Book*. Eugene, OR: Crystalline Publications, 2015.

Patel, Sanjay. *The Little Book of Hindu Deities: From the Goddess of Wealth to the Sacred Cow*. New York: Penguin Random House, 2006.

Pearson, Nicholas. *Stones of the Goddess: 104 Crystals for the Divine Feminine*. Rochester, VT: Destiny Books, 2019.

Penczak, Christopher. *Spirit Allies: Meet Your Team from the Other Side*. San Francisco: Red Wheel/Weiser, 2002.

Reeves, Gene, trans. *The Lotus Sutra*. Somerville, MA: Wisdom Publications, 2008.

Regardie, Israel. *Be Yourself: The Art of Relaxation*. North Haven, CT: Cosmic Eye Publishing, 2018.

Reinhart, Melanie. *Chiron and the Healing Journey*. London: Starwalker Press, 2009.

Scheffer, Mechthild. *The Encyclopedia of Bach Flower Therapy*. Rochester, VT: Healing Arts Press, 2001.

Simmons, Robert, and Naisha Ahsian. *The Book of Stones: Who They Are and What They Teach*. Rochester, VT: Destiny Books, 2005.

Smith, John D. trans. *The Mahabharata*. New York: Penguin Books, 1991.

Stewart, R. J. *Celtic Gods, Celtic Goddesses*. London: Cassell Illustrated, 1992.

———. *Power Within the Land: The Roots of Celtic and Underworld Traditions Awakening the Sleepers and Regenerating the Earth*. Rockport, MA: Element Books, 1992.

Stone, Joshua David. *The Ascended Masters Light the Way: Beacons of Ascension*. Flagstaff, AZ: Light Technology Publishing, 1995.

Tompkins, Sue. *The Contemporary Astrologer's Handbook*. London: Flare Publications, 2006.

Vaudoise, Mallorie. *Honoring Your Ancestors: A Guide to Ancestral Veneration*. Woodbury, MN: Llewellyn Publications, 2021.

Virtue, Doreen. *Archangels and Ascended Masters: A Guide to Working and Healing with Divinities and Deities*. Carlsbad, CA: Hay House, 2004.

Wallace, B. Alan. *The Four Immeasurables: Practices to Open the Heart*. Boston: Shambhala Publications, 1999.

Wilkinson, Richard H. *The Complete Gods and Goddesses of Ancient Egypt*. New York: Thames and Hudson, 2020.

Wooten, Rachel. *Tara: The Liberating Power of the Female Buddha*. Boulder, CO: Sounds True, 2020.

Yogananda, Paramahansa. *Autobiography of a Yogi*. Los Angeles: Self-Realization Fellowship, 2015.

To Write to the Author

If you wish to contact the author or would like more information about this book, please write to the author in care of Llewellyn Worldwide Ltd. and we will forward your request. Both the author and publisher appreciate hearing from you and learning of your enjoyment of this book and how it has helped you. Llewellyn Worldwide Ltd. cannot guarantee that every letter written to the author can be answered, but all will be forwarded. Please write to:

Dawn McLaughlin
℅ Llewellyn Worldwide
2143 Wooddale Drive
Woodbury, MN 55125-2989

Please enclose a self-addressed stamped envelope for reply,
or $1.00 to cover costs. If outside the U.S.A., enclose
an international postal reply coupon.

Many of Llewellyn's authors have websites with additional information and resources. For more information, please visit our website at http://www.llewellyn.com.

Notes